Putting Away Childish Things

Walk as wise and not as fools
Wise men still seek Him

By

Venoris Patten

Copyright ©2012 by Venoris Patten

PUTTING AWAY CHILDISH THINGS

Printed in the United States of America

ISBN 978-0-9852094-9-0

All rights reserved solely by the author. The author guarantees all contents are original and do not infringe upon the legal rights of any other person or work. No part of this book may be reproduced in any form without the permission of the author. The views expressed in this book are not necessarily those of the publisher.

Unless otherwise indicated, Bible quotations are taken from the King James version of the Bible.
Copyright © 1982 by Thomas Nelson.

HOLY BIBLE, NEW INTERNATIONAL VERSION®.
Copyright © 1973, 1978, 1984
by International Bible Society.
Used by permission of
Zondervan Publishing House.

New Living Translation (NLT) Holy Bible.
New Living Translation copyright© 1996, 2004, 2007 by Tyndale House Foundation. Used by permission of Tyndale House Publishers Inc., Carol Stream, Illinois 60188.
All rights reserved.

www.trueperspectivepublishinghouse.com

AUTOGRAPH PAGE

Because of your value; autograph this book to yourself or someone else you value.

> *"When I was a child, I talked like a child; I thought like a child, I reasoned like a child. When I became a man, I put the ways of childhood behind me"*
> *(1 Corinthians 13:11) NIV.*

Acknowledgement

I proudly acknowledge my Lord and Savior Jesus Christ, for the insight and aptitude that He has given to me; enabling me to produce my second book. I recently heard and now really understand the concept of being a co-creator with God. I thank God for His enabling.

I make special mention of my pastor, Bishop Chris Dutruch, senior pastor of celebration of Praise, Clermont Florida. His courage, transparency, and no-nonsense demeanor challenge me to perpetually seek a higher place in Christ, and thus putting away childish things.

I acknowledge my previous pastors and teachers, particularly Dr. Burchell Taylor, Senior pastor of Bethel Baptist Church, Jamaica, West Indies; Dr. Owen Facey, Genesis Christian Center, Ft. Lauderdale Florida; and Dr. Reginald G. Smith – Retired. They have been very instrumental in my spiritual growth over the years.

The Lord has blessed me with some very valuable supporters in and around my life. I assess the people close to me and acknowledge that Yes! I am fortunate to be a part of a "royal priesthood".

FORWARD

The apostle Paul makes it clear in his letter to the Corinthians that there is a direct link between who we become and what we experience. He notes, "***Blessed be God, even the Father of our Lord Jesus Christ, the Father of mercies, and the God of all comfort; Who comforteth us in all our tribulation, that we may be able to comfort them which are in any trouble, by the comfort wherewith we ourselves are comforted of God. 2 Corinthians 1:3-4*** (KJV). This book "Putting Away Childish Things" approaches the reader from that vantage point.

Many times we find teachers and writers trying to teach what they do not know or experience. Such attempts allow the written word to become sterile and the spoken word dry. Venoris Patten, the author of this refreshing work, uses her experiences as a spring board for probing thoughts, while at the same time interweaves powerful biblical concepts into her story. Readers are challenged to think critically about the why of their own experience and encouraged to move to a higher level of maturity.

Scripture is clear that maturity is a process. We do not just suddenly wake up one morning and find ourselves mature, spiritually. It is a daily walk, an ongoing grind, one that is filled with fits and starts. We move from the nadir of human peril to the zenith of spiritual ecstasy. The wisdom in it all is that we do not find maturity at the bottom of the valley neither at the summit of the mountain. Both places lead us to a deeper understanding of ourselves and a greater awareness of the God who spoke to Moses in Ex. 3, saying *Hayeh asir Hayeh* - I will be who I will be. The God who is interested in our maturity is radically free to lead us to the places of his choosing, not necessarily the places for our comfort. As people of God we must find rest in the hands of this God who becomes unpredictable, yet loving, prickly yet comforting, faithful yet testing. The reality is we are not very comfortable with those places, but at the end of the day all God requires of his people is that we trust him and live a life of obedience. I believe this book captures the essence of this God who is madly in love with us but sometimes leads us to places we find challenging and difficult.

My encouragement is to read this book reflectively. Read it prayerfully and in the end let the author's insights propel you to a more profound and serendipitous relationship with God.

Dr. Owen Facey

INTRODUCTION

Over the fifty seven years of my life, I have come to understand that everything in which we are engaged, whatever we become, whatever we strive to be, all involve a process. In every discipline of life, whether physical, social, psychological, emotional or spiritual, or any other area you can imagine, a process of growth is involved.

Studying the stages of growth in mankind substantiate this. The scriptures also instruct us on this in the book of Hebrews and other references. In embracing the process of maturing in Christ we have to come to a place of "putting away childish things" and entertaining the concept of eating "solid meat" i.e. maturing in Christ.

"So let us stop going over the basic teachings about Christ again and again. Let us go on instead and become mature in our understanding. Surely we don't need to start again with the fundamental importance of repenting from evil deeds and placing our faith in God" (Hebrews 6:1) NLT.

"I am writing to you who are mature in the faith because you know Christ, who existed from the beginning. I am writing to you who are young in the faith because you have won your battle with the evil one" (1John 2:13) NLT.

The aim of this book is to enlighten the reader on the deeper truths of "putting away childish things." As we mature in life, we automatically go from one stage to the next, and it follows that we go through various changes in each stage; that is, putting away some things and adopting other more meaningful things. Many of the changes are automatic and others are intentional. The intentional changes should reflect advancement by putting away the childish things of immaturity and "eating solid food" as grown adults.

As you read this book, hopefully you will glean insight into some spiritual truths that took many, many years for me to understand. I pray that there will be a paradigm shift into a new dimension as God enlightens you through His precepts. The awesome thing about God is that He deals with us individually as He sees fit. It might not take the many years that it took me for you to gain the understanding that God desires to lavish on you, but there is a common thread among the people of God who have made a difference in the Kingdom of God. This commonality is periods of "drought" experiences.

The people of God who have made a significant difference in the Kingdom have all gone through great hardships. Ask Abraham, Isaac, Jacob, Moses, Joseph, Paul and Peter.... The Scripture is replete with people of faith who have endured their drought experiences. The reassuring thing is that God goes through it with us, using the adversities to make us the people He has called us to be.

He knows our frame and He knows how much we can bear. Because of this we can live with great expectation and anticipation to see His hand at work. We can be going through days, weeks or years of drought and then suddenly, without warning, God makes a one hundred and eighty degree turn. All of a sudden we are the head and not the tail, we are above and not beneath. So it was with me. I thank God that He considers me worthy and actually gives me His attention.

So do not think that you have to go through fifty seven years to hear from God. You are unique and God deals with you uniquely. God requires us to be steadfast and watchful and to avail ourselves to Him. He is calling us to a purpose-filled life and to achieve this, we have to grow from "stage to stage and glory to glory" **(2Peter 3:18)**. We have to walk as wise and not as fools **(Ephesians 5:14-16)**.

To mature in Christ, we have to get beyond the dos and don'ts of religion and yearn for the true essence of faith in God, and thereby walk by faith. Try to remember this saying; There is **"none so blind as those that will not see"**, Matthew Henry (1662-1714) English Presbyterian minister and writer. It has been refreshing having gone through some recent challenges in my life and to come to a place where I have a greater confidence in God.

The dark experiences reflected in my autobiography "Nuggets…along the Way" tell how my difficulties turned out to be stepping stones in disguise. These experiences have helped to release me from "being entangled with yolks of bondage" and brought me to a purposeful place in God.

I have embraced the concept of putting away childish things and I embrace a growth walk with God. I pray that I have inspired you to take even the first step in this unpopular yet most rewarding direction.

TABLE OF CONTENTS

Chapter one   1
Taking Responsibility

- All the World's a stage Monologue.......1
- My Perspective..............................3
- How it all Began.............................7
- Purpose..9
- Forgiveness..................................13

Chapter two   19
Message of Assurance

- Lessons from Isaiah 40....................22
- Message of Comfort.......................24
- Message for Ministry...................... 25
- Message to Exalt the Lord................27
- Humility.......................................28
- Preparation..................................30
- "Stop Quoting Scriptures and Come alongside people"................... 31
- The True Church..........................35

Chapter three — 37
Faith

- Major Events in Abraham's Life..........38
- Significance of the Altars Abraham built..............................44
- How is your Faith?........................50

Chapter four — 53
Prayer

- My Ocean-like experience at Trinity Broadcasting Network............. 55
- Is there a correct way to pray?............... 57
- Persistence in prayer...................... 58
- Parable of the persistent widow........... 59
- Reasons to pray...........................60
- Other insights in prayer..................61
- God waits on the believers prayer..63
- Discernment through prayer............. 67
- Effective prayers......................... 69

Chapter five — 75
Seasons

- The Winter Season........................77
- Serenity Prayer............................79
- Current Hard Knocks.....................82

Chapter six   89
Life -A Paradox

- Previous concepts on marriage................92
- The paradigm shift..............................93
- Courage...97
- Do I have to be humiliated to be humble?..................................102
- Would God direct a divorce?.........................103
- Would God just sit back and not act on His children's' behalf?...105
- Would God allow His people to sin?...................................106

Chapter seven   111
Encouragement

- Baruch..113
- Anchored to the Rock.............................118

Chapter eight   121
I have begun to deliver... Now begin to possess

- Confirmation.......................................123
- A surrendered life.................................125

Chapter nine 131
If I have found favor in thy sight, then show me thy ways

- A look at Elijah..................................132
- A look at Solomon.............................134
- A look at Moses................................136
- A look at Jesus' relationship with us – His disciples........................140

Chapter ten 143
You were born for this

- It's not about you..............................148
- God can use anything........................149
- King David......................................151
- Paul...153
- God will cause you to soar to high heights..................................155

Chapter eleven 157
Giving ~ A matter of the heart

- How do we give?..............................158
- The Church Community....................159
- Tithing...161
- Abraham and Melchizedeck...............162
- Why was the tithe instituted?............165
- Is the tithe still part of God's program for giving?........................166

CHAPTER 1

∽ Taking Responsibility ∽

"When I was a child, I talked like a child; I thought like a child, I reasoned like a child. When I became a man, I put the ways of childhood behind me"
    (1 Corinthians 13:11) NIV.

Our natural development consists of different stages. Shakespeare, in his Play "As You Like It" describes it in a monologue by the character Melancholy Jacques.

ALL THE WORLD'S A STAGE MONOLOGUE

All the world's a stage,
and all the men and women merely players:
They have their exits and their entrances;
and one man in his time plays many parts,
His acts being seven ages.

At first the infant,
Mewling and puking in the nurse's arms.
And then the whining school-boy, with his satchel
and shining morning face, creeping like snail
unwillingly to school.

*And then the lover,
sighing like furnace, with a woeful ballad
Made to his mistress' eyebrow. Then a soldier,
Full of strange oaths and bearded like the pard,
Jealous in honor, sudden and quick in quarrel,
Seeking the bubble reputation
Even in the cannon's mouth.*

*And then the justice,
in fair round belly with good capon lined,
with eyes severe and beard of formal cut,
Full of wise saws and modern instances;
and so he plays his part. The sixth age shifts
Into the lean and slipper'd pantaloon,
With spectacles on nose and pouch on side,
His youthful hose, well saved, a world too wide
For his shrunk shank; and his big manly voice,
Turning again toward childish treble, pipes
And whistles in his sound. Last scene of all,
that ends this strange eventful history,
is second childishness and mere oblivion,
sans teeth, sans eyes, sans taste, sans everything.*

Throughout our developmental stages there is a seamless transition as we shift gears from one level to the next in our maturity whether physically, mentally, psychologically socially or spiritually. We mature at different rate of speed, however it is expected that each stage of development be achieved within a certain time frame.

Some areas of our development can be quantified, but most of an individual's life is unquantifiable and more qualitative. It is important to note that we never stop developing, unless there is some type of injury, and even when we reach the peak of development and start regressing, change is still taking place.

The physical part of our being, which is the only real quantifiable part and therefore the part that can be readily assessed, is that part that seems to get most attention in terms of development; yet it is the part of least importance in terms of the Spiritual. The other areas, especially the Spiritual, are marginalized and tend to develop by default. That's the reason so many people are grown adults, but function as children. There are many homes where children have to take leadership roles because adult are dysfunctional. They are actually underdeveloped in the areas that matter most.

Psychologists try to shed light on the psychological aspect of a person; social psychologists have guidelines for determining normal behaviors and can tell who falls under the guideline of a sociopath. There are qualifying guidelines for physical maturation, and even Shakespeare illustrated in poetic form, his idea of the functional stages of man in his "All the world's a Stage" monologue. There are many other disciplines that lend a hand in determining the mystery of the human development; in terms of who we are, how we live, growth, purpose, tendencies and so forth.

My Perspective

I wish I could say that I was a great reader or even a very good one. I believe that a good discipline in reading is the gateway to knowledge, and allows us to be conversant with what really matters in the journey of our lives. I lack this discipline. I always struggled with concentration and that struggle has discouraged me as a reader while I was growing up. I had to force myself to read, and even then I would read only enough to satisfy the requirement of passing to the next grade level, or to pass the test.

At that stage of my development, I functioned as a child in terms of my outlook in life. I figured that I would do what was necessary to make it. I did not believe in pushing myself and had no concept of, or saw the need to stretch beyond. I can safely say that as a child my imagination was limited to my immediate environment and not much more. I was unmotivated.

When I became a young adult I started challenging myself as I saw other people achieving great things. I still had an issue with concentration and reading and would have to read paragraphs over again to gain the meaning. I saw people speed-reading and that fascinated me. In college I had to work doubly hard to qualify with my peers, but I determined that even if I had to work twice as hard to be considered half as good, it was still worth it. I took comfort in the fact that the harder one works for something, the more valuable it is to such person. I stayed the course and finished the academic race achieving my master's degree in Health Services Administration. Needless to say I am proud of every milestone I've attained, and everything I have achieved in my life.

Because learning did not come easy to me I am amazed that certain literary references would pop up into my mind, and always at an opportune time. This is one of those times as Shakespeare's character Melancholy Jacque, who I read about in high school forty years ago, rewards me again with the concept that "all the world's a stage and all the men and women merely players." It popped into my mind just at the right time.

I truly believe God is aiding me, even in my weak areas. Now I am discovering writing as a venting tool. It's like exhaling. It's a release of what would otherwise be pent-up. It also helps me to process and to decipher between what is reasonable and sensible and what is foolish. It helps me in determining what to keep and what to discard. My confidence in functioning in my profession as a registered nurse was shaken after receiving chemotherapy a year ago. My concentration and my memory were challenged and I would second guess myself in everything. The newly discovered hobby of writing, which forces me into reading more, has helped me tremendously not only in regaining my confidence, but also in restoring my concentration.

I believe I am in the fifth stage of the Shakespearean Staging profile. I am on the other side of my professional life and getting a glimpse of sixth stage.

Shakespeare said *"the sixth age shifts into the lean and slipper'd pantaloon, with spectacles on nose and pouch on side"*. Is it a welcoming sight? Am I looking forward to the other stages of my development? Yes! Although a little apprehensive, I am looking forward towards every aspects of my life. I have gained confidence as I gain better understanding about my purpose in life.

Putting Away Childish Things

I have to admit that there have been times when I have faced certain difficult situations with trepidation, and wanted to walk in the opposite direction, but I faced my fears and here I am. I can confidently say that every difficulty, hardship, turbulence, pain, sorrow, heartache, or disappointment is an opportunity for advancement in my development. When I was a child I took the easy way out. Now I am grown I have to develop mature and enduring muscles to function like a grown-up. I cannot avoid anymore, I have to face my fears. I am seeing the "good" in bad situations through the lens of experience. I have to put away childish things.

"When I was a child, I talked like a child; I thought like a child, I reasoned like a child. When I became a man, I put the ways of childhood behind me" (1 Corinthians 13:11) NIV.

When I was growing up, my family did not have modern conveniences such as we have today. We had no electricity or running water. We had no built-in toilets, but outhouses which we called latrine. It did not matter to us because everyone in the neighborhood was subjected to the same inconveniences. In fact, it was not an issue. As the saying goes "it is what it is" well I'll now say "it was what it was".

I used to carry buckets of water on my head and sometimes had to go back and forth to the stream many times before going to school in the mornings. All my siblings had different chores and my sisters and I had to make sure the barrel was full of water.

I eventually perfected the skill of carrying the buckets, but initially it was a great challenge. After all! I was a little girl. When I think of it now I want to hug and reassure myself that "it was all good." I also laugh because it is really funny now. I laugh at the fact that it took what seemed like forever to fill the barrel, which was already ¾ full; it was never kept empty.

I had to make many trips because from the stream to the house I would spill almost all my water. After a while, Mom would have mercy on me and let me stop. In spite of the tediousness of life then, those experiences have molded me into someone that endures.

Growth is a natural occurrence in many aspects; however spiritual growth takes intentionality. It's not something that happens by default, but a process that comes about by the unwelcome, unfortunate, disappointing, and distressing experiences of our lives; even some that are sometimes downright disastrous. The Lord turns our tests into a testimony. Read the life of Moses, Job, David, Joseph, Paul… to name a few, and you will see the testament to the fact that trials bring about maturity. **"But we glory in tribulations also: knowing that tribulation worketh patience" (Romans 5:3) KJV.** It is critical for us to endure if we want growth and spiritual maturity. He desires us to be more like Him. He is calling us daily but are we hearing. There is none as blind as those who will not see; there is none as deaf as those who will not hear.

Putting away childish things is mandatory for our spiritual growth. "Childlikeness" refers to a person's temperament. "Childishness" refers to a person's behavior. It's refreshing to maintain a childlike disposition of innocence, trust, and ingeniousness. The Scripture refers to us having childlike faith but admonish us to put away childish things. **"The Lord protects those of childlike faith; I was facing death, and he saved me" (Psalm 116:6) NLT.**

HOW IT ALL BEGAN

Why do children do the same thing over and over in spite of warnings, reprimand and corrections? While we were growing up, my brothers were veterans at getting into trouble and getting a "beating" because they were very strong-willed. I was involved in a few occurrences also but generally I was compliant because I was afraid of "beatings".

As an adult, when I reminisce about my childhood and make a comparison with young people today, I conclude that there is an innate tendency in a child from birth that has the propensity to do the wrong thing. This propensity is called SIN. We all have it and demonstrate it in various ways. Even in adulthood, this tendency to do the wrong over and over is reflected in our society every day. Most of us know how sin began with Adam and Eve. Genesis chapter 3 recounts the story of how man and woman sinned.

Sadly, some people absolutely reject it as fictitious and therefore not worthy of serious thought, however the Bible is the inspired word of God. **"All Scripture is inspired by God and is useful to teach us what is true and to make us realize what is wrong in our lives. It corrects us when we are wrong and teaches us to do what is right"** (2Timothy 3:16) NLT.

The tendency that is in the child from birth, if it is not dealt with adequately, will manifest in adulthood in more demanding, aggressive, manipulative and even hostile ways. The story of Cain and Abel in Genesis chapter 4 reflects the effect of SIN.

"In the course of time Cain brought some of the fruits of the soil as an offering to the LORD. [4] And Abel also brought an offering—fat portions from some of the firstborn of his flock.

The LORD looked with favor on Abel and his offering, ⁵ but on Cain and his offering he did not look with favor. So Cain was very angry, and his face was downcast. Then the LORD said to Cain, "Why are you angry? Why is your face downcast? ⁷ If you do what is right, will you not be accepted? But if you do not do what is right, sin is crouching at your door; it desires to have you, but you must rule over it" (Genesis 4:3-7) NLT.

Cain and Abel had brought offering to God. Abel's was accepted, Cain's was rejected based on the standard that was set for bringing offering to God. Rather than repenting and making it right, Cain started pouting, so God admonished him. It did not stop there; the rest of the story reflects how most people, both children and adults, behave today.

Do you move to correct the mistake or deny that you need to correct it? After Cain's sacrifice was rejected, God gave him the chance to right his wrongs and try again. God even encouraged him to do this! But Cain refused, and the rest of his life is a startling example of what happens to those who refuse to admit their mistakes. Cain eventually murdered his brother.

Now Cain said to his brother Abel, "Let's go out to the field". While they were in the field, Cain attacked his brother Abel and killed him. (Genesis 4:8) NLT.

As we mature, we are required to take responsibility for our behavior. What was excused as a child cannot be excused as an adult, and if it is continually excused that person develops with deficits in functioning as an adult. To the extreme degree, that person who has not learned to take responsibility, becomes a misfit in society and may even become a sociopath, whose behavior is antisocial and who lacks a sense of moral responsibility or social conscience. That is tantamount to being a child. We have to put away childish things as we mature. Taking responsibility for our actions is a sign of maturity.

PURPOSE

So we take responsibility and we mature and become functional members of the society, then what? That's what we are taught to do, but what next? What is it all about? Many people do not see the point to their existence and so they live aimlessly. They go through the motion day by day and feel dissatisfied and unfulfilled at the end of each day. They work daily, pay bills which keep increasing, deal with the creditors, deal with the children, ward off the repo man, and keep doing the same thing over and over again.

When this sense of lack of purpose persists, that person may become reckless, uncaring and irresponsible. As life's testing's and trials continue to confront this person he may become arbitrary, acting out of how he feels at the moment. He may become unreliable, inconsistent and if this negative routine continues, he may downright give up altogether. All this happens because of a lack of purpose in his life.

Purpose as defined by Dictionary.com is:
1. The reason for which something exists or is done, made, used, etc.
2. An intended or desired result; end; aim; goal.
3. Determination; resoluteness.
4. The subject in hand; the point at issue.
5. Practical result, effect, or advantage: *to act to good purpose*

According to Merriam-Webster Dictionary, Purpose is:
  a. Something set up as an object or end to be attained
  b. Resolution, determination
  c. A subject under discussion, or an action in course of execution; by intent-intentionally.

Synonyms: Aim, Ambition, Aspiration, Design, Dream, End, Ideal, Intent, Intention, Mark, Meaning, object, Objective, Plan, Point, Goal, Target.

Having a knowledge, understanding, and acceptance of our purpose in life is a big step to experiencing wellness and contentment. There is an abundance of reasons why we can be discontented in life. From physical and emotional pain, to disappointment in the inequity in our social structure, there are a myriad of reasons why we can be discontented. This is a fact of life; some things we can change and most we cannot because they are out of our direct control.

So! What do we do with the causes of discontentment? The answer is short and simple but not necessarily easy. We have a choice to be content or not, and we can choose to be content. The Apostle Paul faced similar issues and had this advice.

"I rejoiced greatly in the Lord that at last you renewed your concern for me. Indeed, you were concerned, but you had no opportunity to show it. [11] I am not saying this because I am in need, for I have learned to be content whatever the circumstances. [12] I know what it is to be in need, and I know what it is to have plenty. I have learned the secret of being content in any and every situation, whether well fed or hungry,

whether living in plenty or in want" (Philippians 4: 10-12) NLT.

Paul learned the secret of contentment and taught this to the Philippians and is teaching that to us, if we will learn. He further told the church that **"godliness with contentment is great gain. [7] For we brought nothing into the world and we can take nothing out of it"1Timothy 6:6-7) NLT.**

As varied as our concerns in life are so are the opinions on how to deal with them. It is good to follow good teaching and wise council at all stages of our lives. We need to do that, but it behooves us to get to that place of understanding in life where we know that there is purpose in our ups and downs.

In spite of all the good teaching and in spite of the all the "wise" council, it will not hinder or short-circuit the path of pain, heartache and suffering that we have to go through in our journey to our destiny. Gaining wisdom, knowledge and understanding help us to embrace purpose and therefore foster contentment.

In spite of the fact that I have been walking with the Lord for many years, it took a long time for me to come to this place, and still I am not really there. I am still a work in progress. Once I got a sense of this concept though, I am more at peace with myself, other people and the situations that come up ever so often that affect my life. I have learned not to panic over things, but rather to do what I can do about it and give my expectations to God since I know that He will bring me to an expected end.

"My soul, wait thou only upon God; for my expectation is from him." (Psalm 62:5) KJV.

"For I know the thoughts that I think toward you, saith the LORD, thoughts of peace, and not of evil, to give you an expected end" (Jeremiah 29:11) KJV.

This insight on life has given me leverage and helped me to "de-stress". The many times in the past when I would ask the many Whys, are converted to a time and place when I look with expectation for the Lord to show me how it fits into the whole scheme of things; how it fits into the big picture. Sometimes He does not show me either, but I am content to know that He has a plan and what He does is best done. I am content to know that He even talks to me; that He considers me.

To get to this place, I have released and am continually releasing the past painful baggage and I am embracing the present and the future. In doing this, I free myself from the offences of the past only to discover that I have increased capacity to embrace life more fully and even to adventure out into new territories. In other words, I have found that this releasing process is quite liberating.

FORGIVENESS

It is very hard to forgive. Walking in forgiveness is definitely a spiritual concept. The flesh desires so much to walk in offence, to maintain hate, and to look for vengeance. Although I do not remember ever looking for opportunity to take revenge on anyone, I have been guilty of holding grudges and offences. Over the years, the Lord has shown me the importance of forgiveness.

He has shown me that having unforgivenss in my heart is actually a breeding ground for sickness, diseases and premature death while forgiveness brings release, health, healing and wholeness. Forgiveness is even more so for the person forgiving than for the one who committed the wrong.

I did not learn to apply this concept overnight. It has been a process for me, but now I embrace any opportunity that comes for forgiveness. I am not going out searching for hard times in order to show forgiveness; God knows that I prefer an easy life, but I have learnt that everything along my way is opportunity. There are tremendous opportunities daily to practice forgiveness.

December 7th was my birthday. After doing my daily devotion, I asked the Lord to make me a blessing to someone that day. I was sad in heart because of my dysfunctional marriage and I surrendered it to the Lord as I have done many other times. I then went to the Church, called the visitors who had visited the past Sunday and encouraged and prayed with many of them. As I got involved in people's lives my sadness disappeared and I was praising God.

The best part of my day came at the end of the day when I went to the fish shop. In interacting with the worker there the Lord showed me a great need and gave me the chance to minister. The man was hurting because his wife had run off with another man and left him broke.

Thankfully, the store was not busy and he was able to talk at length and I listened. He said that he could not wait to see her in a gutter somewhere suffering. To this I suggested to him to pray for his wife and to forgive her instead. He looked at me in astonishment and said:

"Me? No way".

I told him that only God is able to free him from the deep pain that he was experiencing and I explained the forgiveness principle drawing reference to Joseph's life (Genesis 37-42). I then offered to pray for him and he agreed. He was tearful after I prayed and the Lord nudged me to offer Salvation to Him. I hesitated thinking that anyone could walk into the store at anytime, but the Lord urged me. The man accepted the Lord as his personal Savior and Lord and is excited about connecting in fellowship with the believers.

"So watch yourselves! If another believer sins, rebuke that person; then if there is repentance, forgive. Even if that person wrongs you seven times a day and each time turns again and asks forgiveness, you must forgive. The apostles said to the Lord, "Show us how to increase our faith" (Luke 17:3-5) NLT.

"Work at living in peace with everyone, and work at living a holy life, for those who are not holy will not see the Lord. ^{15} Look after each other so that none of you fails to receive the grace of God. Watch out that no poisonous root of bitterness grows up to trouble you, corrupting many. ^{16} Make sure that no one is immoral or godless like Esau, who traded his birthright as the firstborn son for a single meal" (Hebrews 12:14-16).

The best of us have our struggles that puzzle us. Our humanness automatically spells trouble. **"How frail is humanity! How short is life, how full of trouble! (Job 14:1) NLT.** There is divine purpose in our troubles. Our problems and human limitations have many benefits.

- They remind us of Christ's suffering
- They keep us from pride

- They cause us to look beyond this brief life
- They give us opportunity to prove our faith to others
- They give God the opportunity to demonstrate His power

These issues of our lives are our outer man dying. We struggle to constantly revive and resuscitate the outer man, but we need instead to dig deep into the Spirit, that is **"being renewed daily"** to get our strength for the journey. So get your strength from the Spirit man and be revived.

"That is why we never give up. Though our bodies are dying, our spirits are being renewed every day. For our present troubles are small and won't last very long. Yet they produce for us a glory that vastly outweighs them and will last forever!"(2 Corinthians 4: 16-17) NLT.

Although we have the assurance of the promises of God for our lives, we do get disappointed, let down, downcast and saddened because our emotions are naturally responding. God gave us feelings and we respond to the pain and irritations inflicted on us. As we grow in grace, our response changes from natural to Spiritual. That is why we can forgive; and in forgiving we find release, deliverance and freedom.

My daughter-in-law encouraged me last night. She said that *"while sadness can coexist with peace bitterness cannot coexist with peace."* So I choose to forgive so no seed of bitterness will spring up. As I digested this further, I realize that sadness is a feeling that comes and goes according to the changing of circumstances, but bitterness is a Spiritual stronghold. Bitterness is like a grown tree from a seed of offence. That is why it is critical to forgive as quickly as possible instead of holding on to offence. I understand that I can have the peace of God and yet be sad; about my child being sick for example. I cannot have the peace of God and be walking in unforgiveness and bitterness.

Bitterness will over-run the peace of God, just like thorns and thistles overrun a field. **"When the ground soaks up the falling rain and bears a good crop for the farmer, it has God's blessing.** [8] But **if a field bears thorns and thistles, it is useless. The farmer will soon condemn that field and burn it"** (Hebrews 6:7-8) NLT.

I have watched how easily weeds overtake the yard and how thorns strangle the flower bed. Why can't the grass out-do the weeds or the flowers out-do the thorns? Why can't Peace out-do bitterness? But, Ah! I realize that because of Sin there is a natural decline that takes place. Because of Sin leaves now fall from the trees, there is problems in relationships, people get sick, and there is death. I also realize that there is a remedy for this decline. Just like there is a natural antidote for natural ailments, there is a Spiritual antidote for Spiritual ailments. The direct remedy for Spiritual ailment of bitterness is the Spiritual remedy of forgiveness.

Chapter 2

❧ Message of Assurance ❧

On 10/27/11 Mary came to my house with a message. I wondered who this person was when my husband came in from the garage to say that there was a woman outside to see me. I went to the door and was about to go out to her, but she was advancing towards me with what seemed like an intent to be invited in.

She was strolling her granddaughter and this scenario jarred my memory to the occasion about a year and a half ago when I was walking through my neighborhood and stopped briefly to talk with Mary. I distinctly remembered because we were not able to understand each other well at that time. You see, I speak English and she speaks Portuguese. Mary had the same vivacious, winning countenance that I had seen before.

I invited Mary in and after the preliminary greeting, which was already a struggle, I did not know what to say or do next, but she did.

"Me Christian, you Christian?" she asked

"Yes I am" I said excitedly

"The Lord send me... you" pointing from the heaven to herself and then to me.

All this was said in very broken English and I was struggling to understand. Although it wasn't going very easily, I was aware that this was a defining moment and that I needed to take heed.

"You have Bibla?" Mary continued

"Yes, I have Bibla", that I understood to be Bible. I ran upstairs to my office and got my Bible. When I got back downstairs, she had gotten her Bible out from under the stroller and was thumbing through the leaves.

"Isaiah" she said while turning to Isaiah chapter forty. I found Isaiah forty in my translation and started reading from the beginning. As I read I was overcome with the awesome awareness of the favor of God on my life.

ISAIAH 40

[1] "**Comfort, comfort my people,**" **says your God.** [2] "**Speak tenderly to Jerusalem. Tell her that her sad days are gone and her sins are pardoned. Yes, the LORD has punished her twice over for all her sins.**"

[3] **Listen! It's the voice of someone shouting, "Clear the way through the wilderness for the LORD! Make a straight highway through the wasteland for our God!** [4] **Fill in the valleys, and level the mountains and hills. Straighten the curves, and smooth out the rough places.** [5] **Then the glory of the LORD will be revealed, and all people will see it together. The LORD has spoken!"**

⁶ A voice said, "Shout!" I asked, "What should I shout?" Shout that people are like the grass. Their beauty fades as quickly as the flowers in a field. ⁷ The grass withers and the flowers fade beneath the breath of the LORD. And so it is with people. ⁸ The grass withers and the flowers fade, but the word of our God stands forever".

⁹ O Zion, messenger of good news, shout from the mountaintops! Shout it louder, O Jerusalem. Shout, and do not be afraid. Tell the towns of Judah, "Your God is coming!" ¹⁰ Yes, the Sovereign LORD is coming in power. He will rule with a powerful arm. See, he brings his reward with him as he comes. ¹¹ He will feed his flock like a shepherd. He will carry the lambs in his arms, holding them close to his heart. He will gently lead the mother sheep with their young……

²⁶ Look up into the heavens. Who created all the stars? He brings them out like an army, one after another, calling each by its name. Because of his great power and incomparable strength, not a single one is missing. ²⁷ O Jacob, how can you say the LORD does not see your troubles? O Israel, how can you say God ignores your rights?²⁸ Have you never heard? Have you never understood? The LORD is the everlasting God, the Creator of all the earth. He never grows weak or weary. No one can measure the depths of his understanding. ²⁹ He gives power to the weak and strength to the powerless.

³⁰ Even youths will become weak and tired, and young men will fall in exhaustion. ³¹ But those who trust in the LORD will find new strength. They will soar high on wings like eagles. They will run and not grow weary. They will walk and not faint."

What I was reading was great words of comfort and reassurance, and the fact that God consider me so greatly that He orchestrated such an unusual plan to bring a message to me was doubly rewarding. The Lord did not use a friend or family member, He did not use a prayer partner or another member from the church, He did not use the Pastor or a counselor, He did not use a co-worker or someone I see regularly. God used someone from another culture and another language to bring a message that came to me as clear as day, in spite of our apparent inadequacies in communication. What a mighty God we serve.

LESSONS LEARNED FROM ISAIAH 40

- Isaiah 40 talks about the restoration of Jerusalem after the exile. I too claim restoration.
- Israel still had 70 more years of exile to go through, so God instructed Isaiah to speak tenderly to Jerusalem and to comfort her. I too claim comfort from God.
- The seeds of comfort may be rooted in the soil of adversity. We may not be able to escape adversity, but we can find God's comfort as we face it. I too look to God and take comfort from Him. Do not ask to escape adversity, but ask God for the Strength to go through it.
- Preparing a straight, smooth, road means removing obstacles and rolling out the red carpet for the coming of the Lord. I make all effort to put out the red carpet for my God. I am not immune to the valleys, hills, and rough places but under God, my faith will not be hindered by them.
- The desert is a picture of life's trials and sufferings. Isaiah told the people to prepare to see God work. I am grateful for God's hand at work in my life and continue to wait expectantly for Him in my situations.

- Verses 6-8. Describe people as grass and the flower of grass that will pass away. In the same way public opinion changes and is unreliable, and will pass away. God's word is unchanging and will last forever. Only in God's eternal Word will we find lasting solution to our problems. I hold on to the Word of God.
- Verse 11. God is often pictured as a shepherd, gently caring for and guiding the flock. He is powerful (40:10), yet caring and gentle. He is called a shepherd (Psalm 23); the good shepherd (John 10:11, 14); the great shepherd (Hebrews 13:20); and the head shepherd (1Peter 5:4). Note that the shepherd is caring for the most defenseless members of the society. I too will look out for the marginalized members of the community and follow His example by caring for them.
- Isaiah describes God's power to create, His provision to sustain, and His presence to help. God is Almighty and all-powerful; but even so He cares for each of us personally. He has proved His care for me.
- Verse 29-31. Even the strongest people get tired and faint at times, but God's power and strength never fails. When life's pressures are crushing in on us we can call on God to renew our strength.
- Vs 31. Talks about waiting on the Lord. It means to completely trust the Lord. What do we do when we come to the end of our faith? We must simply surrender all, even our waning faith, and simply trust Him. As we do this we will experience His strength being made perfect in our weakness. Jesus responding to Paul after Paul went to Him three times with the same adversity said **"My grace is sufficient for thee: for my strength is made perfect in weakness. Most gladly therefore will I**

rather glory in my infirmities, that the power of Christ may rest upon me" (2 Corinthians 12: 9) KJV.

This message given to me that day has caused me to take a more deliberate look on Isaiah 40. I see this chapter in a new light and no more will I gloss over it. I see three segments to the chapter.

- ## MESSAGE OF COMFORT

Verses 1-5 come as a message of comfort to me, Venoris Patten, and it's an invitation to whoever will receive it as a personal message. It reassures me that my sad days are over. I have felt at times, that I have received double hardship in my most recent experiences.

I am sure that many of you have experienced this dilemma in suffering too. Does it mean that there will be no more sad days for me? No! It means that the trials that have been besetting me have not gone unnoticed by God. He hears and answers prayer and knows how and when to set wrongs things right.

The Prophet Isaiah was sent with a message of comfort for Israel. The world is full of hurting people and we, the children of God, have been sent with a message of comfort for them. Before we can be competent to deliver this message, we have to be trained. The training ground for the message of Comfort is Adversity.

You have to be wounded and experience the binding up of your wounds by the great physician Jesus, before you are ready to give first aid treatment to the wounded. Do you have questions about the adversities that you are going through? Welcome it as opportunity. I am learning the lesson even as I am writing this page. I see the picture that it is a stepping stone for greater advancement in ministry.

"All praise to God, the Father of our Lord Jesus Christ. God is our merciful Father and the source of all comfort. [4] He comforts us in all our troubles so that we can comfort others. When they are troubled, we will be able to give them the same comfort God has given us. [5] for the more we suffer for Christ, the more God will shower us with his comfort through Christ." (2 Corinthians 1: 3-5) NLT

> *God comforts us not to make us comfortable but to make us comforters* – John Henry Jowett

- **MESSAGE FOR MINISTRY**

Verses 6-11 point me to ministry work. It cautions me to take heed and respond to the invitation to testify of what God has done for me and to seek to win souls. The instruction to clear the way, make a straight pathway, fill the valleys, level the hills and mountains, and to make the rough places smooth is a direction to prepare people, not just to live for God now, but to be ready for Christ's second coming. I endeavor to make use of every opportunity to win souls, to encourage hearts and to affirm people; in essence to be an Encourager and to do the work of evangelism.

I particularly like the story of Daniel and his great example on complete commitment to God in ministry. Daniel found favor with King Darius and was made overseer over all the administrators, prefects, princes, advisers, and other officials in the Kingdom of Persia. They were jealous of his position and convened a plot against him. They manipulated the King to sign a decree that that specifically opposed Daniel's prayer practice to God. Daniel did not compromise, but stayed faithful to God and the King was forced against his desire to throw Daniel into the lion's den according to the decree that he, the King, had previously sign.

Tormented all night about Daniel, the King arose early in the morning and ran to the den and called out in anguish **"Daniel, servant of the living God! Was your God, whom you serve so faithfully, able to rescue you from the lions?" (Daniel 6:20)** NLT. Daniel replied humbly and wisely acknowledging the King's position and yet reverencing God.

Daniel answered, "Long lives the king! ²² My God sent his angel to shut the lions' mouths so that they would not hurt me, for I have been found innocent in his sight. And I have not wronged you, Your Majesty" (Daniel 6: 21-22) NLT.

Because of Daniel's faithfulness to God, to the King, and to the people that he served, God granted Daniel favor. This pagan King liked Daniel and had even come to believe that Israel's God was real because of the faithfulness of Daniel and his friends. Now King Darius was also convinced of God's power because He rescued His faithful servant.

Although Daniel was captive in a strange land, his devotion to God was a testimony to powerful rulers such as the King. I daresay that Daniel's life was a testimony before people everyday and served to blaze a Highway for God, as demonstrated in the next verses.

"Then King Darius sent this message to the people of every race and nation and language throughout the world: "Peace and prosperity to you!

"I decree that everyone throughout my kingdom should tremble with fear before the God of Daniel.

For he is the living God, and he will endure forever. His kingdom will never be destroyed, and his rule will never end. [27] He rescues and saves his people; he performs miraculous signs and wonders in the heavens and on earth. He has rescued Daniel from the power of the lions."

[28] So Daniel prospered during the reign of Darius and the reign of Cyrus the Persian" (Daniel 6:25-28) NLT.

Oh! That my life would be such that it testifies of God daily, without me having to preach to people. Such was Daniel's life. He preached without saying a word. May the Lord find me faithful.

- **MESSAGE TO EXALT THE LORD**

Verses 12-31 direct me to the awesomeness of God. The verses talk about the inequality of God. He has no equal. He is marvelous in His work, none can advise Him, He has no need for instruction, He is just and righteous. There is no one that can be compared to Him. "He picks up the whole earth as though it was a grain of sand."

[25] "To whom will you compare me? Who is my equal?" asks the Holy One.

²⁶ Look up into the heavens. Who created all the stars? He brings them out like an army, one after another, calling each by its name. Because of his great power and incomparable strength, not a single one is missing."

I will admit that I am limited in my understanding of how awesome the Lord is. How can I truly grasp the magnitude of His vastness and His love and mercy to His Children? I vow to praise Him and continually strive to bask in His awesome presence. There are people who God has used in awesome ways, not just in years gone by but also in this present time.

As I contemplate how wonderful it is to serve God and to be used of Him, I remember a statement that I read not too long ago; "There is a thin line between being confident that you are relying on God's power and becoming proud because God has used you to achieve great things." Why does this come to me at this time? Maybe to keep me grounded because God is speaking into my life in a new way lately. I am honored that God even considers me. The fact that He is inspiring me to write is beyond me; so this statement is very applicable to me.

HUMILITY

"The Lord resists the proud, but gives grace to the humble" (James 4:6).

One of the cures for evil desires is humility. Pride makes us self-centered and leads us to conclude that we deserve all we can see, touch or imagine. It creates greedy appetites for far more than we need, because we have to compete with and outdo others who have more. We can be relived from self-centered desires by humbling ourselves before God, realizing that all we need is His approval. When the Holy Spirit fills us, we see that this world's seductive attractions are only cheap substitutes for what God has to offer.

"Pride goes before destruction and haughtiness before a fall. It is better to live humbly with the poor than to share plunder with the proud" (Proverbs 16:18-19) NLT.

Proud people take little account of their weaknesses and do not anticipate stumbling blocks. They think they are above the frailties of the common people. In this state of mind they are usually tripped up. Ironically, proud people seldom realize that pride is their problem, although everyone around them is well aware of it. It behooves us to ask someone that we trust whether self-satisfaction has blinded us to the warning signs of pride. We might be helped before the fall.

"In the same way, you younger men must accept the authority of the elders. And all of you serve each other in humility, for God opposes the proud but favors the humble. So humble yourselves under the mighty power of God, and at the right time he will lift you up in honor" (1 Peter 5:5-6).

Both young and old can benefit from Peter's instructions here. Pride often keeps older people from trying to understand young people and keeps young people from listening to those who are older. Peter told both young and old to be humble and serve each other. Young men should follow the leadership of older men, who should lead by example. Respect those who are older than you, listen to those younger than you, and be humble enough to admit that you can learn from others.

We often worry about our position and status, hoping to get proper recognition for what we do. But Peter advises us to remember that God's recognition counts more than human praise. God is able and willing to bless us according to His timing. Humbly obey God regardless of present circumstances, and in His good time – either in this life or the next – He will honor you.

Do you struggle with pride vs. humility like I do? How do you respond when you are unjustly treated? When you are passed over and left feeling slighted? When you are not acknowledged and obviously ignored? How do you respond when you are disrespected? When you feel like you deserve better or you feel cheated? Do you feel that others should stop and listen to you? Do you always feel that life owes you something? Do you feel like everyone else is wrong and you are right? Are you able to say "I am sorry"? Are you able to ask for forgiveness? Are you able to acknowledge that you cause hurt to someone else, or do you rationalized it away? Could you be struggling like I am struggling with some of these questions?

The Lord has been slowing me down, causing me to take long, deep introspective looks at myself and I am excited about that. I am just glad that He spends the time with me. He is still working on me to make me what I ought to be. That He speaks to me in visions, through experiences, through His word, and even sent an angel to me in the form of Mary on October 27th gives me great reassurance that I am favored by God.

PREPARATION

Looking back over my life I can see that the Lord has always been preparing me for ministry. I believe that the experiences along the way, good and bad, have been a part of my preparation and also a part of my ministry itself. I will admit that I have had many missed opportunities.

At this point I am more acutely aware of my role in the kingdom and I am more sensitive to the opportunities as they come along. There have been many defining moments in my life and hindsight confirms that the Lord had been there all the time, weaving the web of my life and bringing me into purpose.

As referenced in my previous book *Nuggets along the Way*, **"Purpose is not a destination reached but a series of opportunities along life's journey that present themselves to us to be in position physically, mentally, and spiritually to fulfill a need that destiny has placed before us, that will serve our fellow man and glorify God."** I particularly like this quote because it holds a great depth of truth that I now embrace daily.

I remember the times not too long ago when my life was arbitrary and non-purposeful, but what a difference now that I understand and live in purpose. Although I am still learning as I go along, I now experience a greater degree of satisfaction, even in the simple things I do. My greatest satisfaction comes when I am aware that the Lord is speaking to me, even if it is in a denial or a waiting pattern. It satisfies me to experience His direct response.

"STOP QUOTING SCRIPTURES AND COME ALONGSIDE PEOPLE".

Recently I was on my way to do my assignment at the Church and as I turned the corner to get onto the church campus, I heard the words "Stop Quoting Scriptures and come alongside people" in my head. It was so loud and so real that I turned to see who was talking. Then I started laughing within myself. I wondered what it meant because as far as I was concerned, it did not apply to me.

I have always been a pragmatist. I always look for the practical side of things. I am also very analytical and tend to reason too much, to my own detriment at times. This tendency was my weakness when I came to accept the Lord as my personal Savior and Lord. I struggled with trying to understand before I would accept; but thank God for the day I accepted Jesus Christ by faith, without understanding what it all entailed. Now I continue on my faith walk with still much to understand, but coming into clarity as Christ illuminates my steps ever so slowly, one step at a time.

"For the Lord is the Spirit, and wherever the Spirit of the Lord is, there is freedom. [18] So all of us who have had that veil removed can see and reflect the glory of the Lord. And the Lord—who is the Spirit—makes us more and more like him as we are changed into his glorious image"(2Corinthians 3:17-18) NLT.

So, that day when I heard those I laughed in my Spirit. I was reasoning with myself about this when I met my friend who I had an appointment with that day. I expressed to her that lately it seemed like the Lord was putting some unusual and unpopular things in my Spirit. As I spoke with her I realized that these things would probably puzzle and even oppose the traditional, mainstream believers.

Days after this experience I was still thinking about it and asking the Lord what else He wanted me to do seeing that I am already doing the job of being an Encourager, which involves coming alongside people on a one to one basis. It was then that I realized that the statement that was put into my Spirit was really a reflection of the Church in general. You see! Just like the success of our nation lies in the grass root entrepreneurs, so also the Spiritual success of our Church and our nation is built on each individual's Spiritual life.

While we listen to great preaching, listen to great gospel songs, go to many conventions, concerts, and retreats, the stark reality is that people who are dealing with pain and the harshness of life need encouragement. True encouragement lies in Caring. People need to know that someone cares. Real care is shown in listening and empathizing. Easily hurting people get lost in the crowd and therefore need someone who is willing to take the time to notice them, to listen to them and to empathize with them. Hurting people need caring people.

The ministry of Encouragement is very necessary and is most effective when done on a one to one basis. Even the Body of Christ is starving for real Encouragers today. Will you commit yourself to start encouraging people? Each one encourages one.

My experience in Christendom has led me to conclude that many of us use the Scriptures as a cop out. No doubt the Scriptures are the written word of God given under the inspiration of the Holy Spirit. **"All scripture is given by inspiration of God, and is profitable for doctrine, for reproof, for correction, for instruction in righteousness"** (2 Timothy 3: 16) KJV.

"For the message God delivered through angels has always stood firm, and every violation of the law and every act of disobedience was punished. [3] So what makes us think we can escape if we ignore this great salvation that was first announced by the Lord Jesus himself and then delivered to us by those who heard him speak? [4] And God confirmed the message by giving signs and wonders and various miracles and

gifts of the Holy Spirit whenever he chose" (Hebrews 2: 2-4) KJV.

Many times we over-spiritualize situations by quoting the Scriptures rather than giving a helping hand to people. There is a time and place for all things. **"For everything there is a season, a time for every activity under heaven" (Ecclesiastes 3:1) NLT.** If a person is starving for physical food and this immediate need is not met, more than likely he will not be able to receive Spiritual food.

Too often we use beautifully coined words of Scriptures to hinder us from helping people in need. I know that there is a thin line between being an enabler and being a help. It is easy to enable people who do not want to help themselves, but I am sure that if we slow down long enough to listen to people, we will be able to determine the difference, under the guidance of the Holy Spirit. My experience as a Registered Nurse for years, have taught me that many times people mostly need someone who cares enough to listen.

The Church, like the world is very busy. We are busy with the routine demands of life; programs, ambitious ventures, more programs, and basically caught up in the natural demands of life so much so that we seem to forget the fundamental purpose why we exist. Church buildings are as overbuilt as our houses are overbuilt, and we run around struggling to pay the mortgage.

We are caught up in the new and improved version of everything. I sense that the Lord is displeased with the Church. We must repent and ask Him forgiveness and return to our Purpose. We exist to **"Love the Lord your God with all your heart and with all your soul and with all your strength and with all your mind and, Love your neighbor as yourself" (Luke**

10:27) **NLT**. We have been caught up in trying to get what is bigger and better at all cost and the **"Lord and the neighbor"** are left out.

The True Church

I am not a theologian or even a brilliant scholar regarding Church or Church history, but I qualify to speak on the basic elements of the Church as described in the Scripture. The Church, the Body of Christ is described in 1 Peter as **"you are a chosen people. You are royal priests, a holy nation, and God's very own possession. As a result, you can show others the goodness of God, for he called you out of the darkness into his wonderful light (1Peter 2:9) NLT.**

So we are God's choice possession, called for a particular purpose. We are called to be God's representatives in this world. We are called to show His Goodness. How can we show His Goodness unless we come alongside people who need His Goodness? Our purpose is the same purpose Jesus spoke to His disciples about in **Mark 16: 15 "Go into all the world and preach the Good News to everyone" NLT.**

Beyond preaching to people, Jesus set many examples to His disciples and to us today to follow. One such example was His interrogation of Peter.

"After breakfast Jesus asked Simon Peter, "Simon son of John, do you love me more than these?"

"Yes, Lord," Peter replied, **"you know I love you."**

"Then feed my lambs," Jesus told him.

[16] **Jesus repeated the question: "Simon son of John, do you love me?"**

"Yes, Lord," Peter said, "you know I love you."

"Then take care of my sheep," Jesus said.

[17] **A third time he asked him, "Simon son of John, do you love me?"**

Peter was hurt that Jesus asked the question a third time. He said, "Lord, you know everything. You know that I love you."

Jesus said, "Then feed my sheep" (John 21: 15-17) NLT.

This is a challenge for all of us to go beyond the quick superficial answer and search our own hearts to see if we really love the Lord. This is deep soul searching. Peter got the point by the third time around. The Lord in essence said to Peter; Are you even my friend? He is saying the same to us. Are we even His friend? And if so; then feed my people.

Chapter 3

❧ Faith ❦

"Faith is the confidence that what we hope for will actually happen; it gives us assurance about things we cannot see" (Hebrews 11:1) NLT.

Our walk with God requires us to walk by faith and not by sight. The scriptures say that without faith it is impossible to please God.

"And it is impossible to please God without faith. Anyone who wants to come to him must believe that God exists and that he rewards those who sincerely seek him" (Hebrews 11:6).

I am encouraged by many Bible characters and Abraham is one of the chief. God singled him out and described him as the father of faith. In studying his life one gets new hope and encouragement because, in spite of the weaknesses and flaws, he still pleased God because of his faith. Isn't it gratifying to know that God does not despise imperfection, but He rewards faithfulness. Abraham was faithful.

MAJOR EVENTS IN ABRAHAM'S LIFE

In Gen: 12 we see God calling Abraham to move from Ur of the Chaldees to an unknown place. God told him to leave his country, and relatives in order to become the father of a nation, and form this nation other nations would be blessed. He left with his wife Sarah, nephew Lot, servants, and livestock and eventually arrived in Canaan, after enduring severe difficulties and tediousness along the way. Israel, the nation that would come from Abraham, was to follow God and influence those with whom they came in contact. Through Abraham's family tree, Jesus was born to save humanity.

Soon after the call, there was a famine in the land and Abraham took Sarah into Egypt. There he lied because of fear for his life, thinking that the people would kill him and take Sarah if they presented as man and wife; so he told Pharaoh that Sarah was his sister. This caused Pharaoh and his household to be plagued by God because Sarah was taken into Pharaoh's harem. Abraham's decision to go into Egypt when faced with famine, and the decision to lie to Pharaoh showed lack of faith and a decline in morals.

This led to him being escorted out of Egypt in public disgrace. Later on in Genesis: 20 we find that Abraham deceived another King, King Abimelech, again lying that Sarah was his sister. Here we see the human tendencies when we operate without the leading of God:
- Although a great man of faith, he showed weakness at these times.
- Abraham was actually developing a habit of lying.
- He dishonored his wife in order to ascertain his personal safety when in trouble.

- He set a bad example for his son Isaac, who copied the same tactics of lying and sacrificing his wife later.

After a while there was a dispute between Abraham's servants and Lot's servants. Abraham took the initiative to resolve the dispute, addressing it with Lot. He allowed Lot first choice in the land and settling with what was left. In this he used unselfishness and kindness in putting family peace above his personal desires. In time war broke out and Lot was captured. His uncle Abraham had to rescue him. Here we learn a few good qualities of Abraham's character:
- He was courageous
- As a leader, he kept himself and his men prepared.
- He did not hold offence against Lot, but forgave him
- He showed preference to Lot in allowing him the best part of the land

On the way back from his victory, Abraham was blessed by Melchizedek, king of Salem. In gratitude Abraham tithed one tenth of what he had captured. This was the first time tithe was mentioned in the scriptures. In honor to God, he also refused to take gifts from the king of Sodom. He said lest when he became wealthy, the king of Sodom would take the credit. We see the strength of Abraham here:
- Before God called Abraham, he was an idol worshipper, yet without being specifically taught the principle of tithing, he initiated it out of gratitude to God and under inspiration of the Holy Spirit.
- In spite of his human failings, Abraham honored God. He did not want anyone, including the King of Sodom, to take God's glory when he became rich.

In spite of his wealth, Abraham was unfulfilled without a son. He asked what was the point of his blessings since he did not have an heir to inherit it. God showed him the heavens and the stars and promised that his descendants would be as innumerable. In Genesis 15:4 God promised him a son.

Abraham believed God and it was accounted to him for righteousness yet a few sentences later he was asking how he could be sure that God would give him a son. He showed his humanness in wanting confirmation. At this God asked him to sacrifice animals, showed him a terrifying vision, and told him that his descendants would be enslaved for 400 years. It is better to obey God the first time around.

"Some time later, the Lord spoke to Abram in a vision and said to him, "Do not be afraid, Abram, for I will protect you, and your reward will be great."

² But Abram replied, "O Sovereign Lord, what good are all your blessings when I don't even have a son? Since you've given me no children, Eliezer of Damascus, a servant in my household, will inherit all my wealth. ³ You have given me no descendants of my own, so one of my servants will be my heir."

⁴ Then the Lord said to him, "No, your servant will not be your heir, for you will have a son of your own who will be your heir." ⁵ Then the Lord took Abram outside and said to him, "Look up into the sky and count the stars if you can. That's how many descendants you will have!"

⁶ And Abram believed the Lord, and the Lord counted him as righteous because of his faith.

⁷ Then the LORD told him, "I am the LORD who brought you out of Ur of the Chaldeans to give you this land as your possession".

⁸ But Abram replied, "O Sovereign LORD, how can I be sure that I will actually possess it?" Genesis 15: 1-8) NLT.

Sometimes it is best to just take God at His word rather than to ask for proof. However He loves us even in our times of doubt. As you read to the end of the chapter, you will see that God granted him his request for proof. God asked Abraham to get a sacrifice of a heifer, a female goat, a ram, a turtledove and a pigeon, all three years old. After he killed them and placed them on the altar, he had to stay and guard it all day long, because the vultures threatened to devour the sacrifice, but Abraham chased them away.

At the end of the evening, Abraham fell into a deep sleep and saw a terrible vision. This was when God said: **"You can be sure that your descendants will be strangers in a foreign land, where they will be oppressed as slaves for 400 years. ¹⁴ But I will punish the nation that enslaves them, and in the end they will come away with great wealth. ¹⁵ As for you, you will die in peace and be buried at a ripe old age"** (Genesis 15:13-15) NLT.

- Like Abraham, we must guard the altar of sacrifice. Imagine guarding all day. It takes a person of great faith and endurance to do this.
- There are always vultures, even at the altar
- The sacrifice attracts the vultures

At age 86 Abraham was still without child and he passively accepted Sarah's suggestion to sleep with Hagar to get his heir, showing lack of faith on both their parts. They were acting in line with the custom of the day; however their disobedience in not waiting on God has led to a whole series of problems even to the present day unrest in the Middle East.

Genesis 16:15 reads that Hagar gave Abraham a son named Ishmael; and Abraham was eighty six years old at the time. After that there was unrest in the household for thirteen long years, so much so that Hagar had to be dismissed.

Abraham was passive and showed poor judgment in leading his family as reflected in his sleeping with Sarah's maid Hagar at Sarah's request, and then sending her away later, again at Sarah's request. He loved his wife dearly and wanted to please her, but this did not excuse his disobedience to God. There is no account that God visited Abraham within the thirteen years, from Hagar's conception, until Genesis 17:1 when Abraham was ninety nine years old.

"When Abram was ninety-nine years old, the LORD appeared to him and said, "I am El-Shaddai—'God Almighty.' Serve me faithfully and live a blameless life. ² I will make a covenant with you, by which I will guarantee to give you countless descendants" Genesis 17:1 NLT.

When Abraham was ninety nine years old God renewed his covenant with him as a father of many nations and sealed it with the requirement that each male child must be circumcised. His name at this point was changed from Abram to Abraham and his wife's from Sarai to Sarah.

He bowed but laughed in disbelief, another occasion where we see a struggle in faith. (**Genesis 17:17**). Some time elapsed and again three angels came to Abraham's camp to reconfirm that Sarah would have a son a year from then. At this Sarah doubted, laughed and lied that she laughed (**Genesis 18:12, 15**).

Abraham was an intercessor. He showed great concern for the lost people in Sodom and Gomorrah, and when God wanted to destroy them he interceded on their behalf. Did Abraham change God's mind staying in intercession and pleading the people's case, asking to spare the city if there were ten innocent souls?

Did he wear God down by negotiating from fifty people down to ten? No! The more likely answer is that God changed Abraham's mind. Abraham knew that God is just and does not frown on sin, but He punishes sin. Abraham might have wondered about God's mercy. He left this conversation with God convinced that God is both kind and fair and indeed merciful. (**Genesis 18:16-33**).

When the son of promise, Isaac was born, Abraham was 100 years old. He kept his pledge to God in circumcising his son, as was now customary, and was able to raise his son to an age of maturity. In honor to God and duty to his son, Abraham sought and found a suitable wife for him. He sent his servant, Eliezer back to the homeland, instead of allowing his son to marry a local girl, which would have been easier. He made his obedience to God full and complete in choosing the "who" and "from where" in regards to his son's wife. We see the character of Abraham playing out in the attitude of his servant Eliezer. This is seen in his prayer to God in choosing the right woman for Isaac (**Genesis 24:12**). He had learned about faith and about God from his master, a reflection of the type of example Abraham set.

Towards the end of his life, Abraham made the appropriate and necessary arrangement for his family's interment and mourned the death of his wife. He subsequently married Keturah, had 6 more children, and made the customary allotment to them with Isaac his promised son being his heir. In spite of the dysfunction within his family, in respect to Hagar's son Ishmael, and Sarah's son Isaac, they both went together to bury their father. This reflected the caliber of father Abraham was.

Abraham was far from being perfect, but he was faithful. Abraham believed God and responded to His voice when he was called out of his country. He started from very humble beginnings. He moved out of his comfort zone willing to go to an unknown city, trusting in an unknown God. When the difficulties of life confronted him, the frailty of his humanness became evident. He was consumed with fear, lied and started practicing lying, and neglected to consistently manage his family. How did he go from a fearful man to "the father of faith?" In studying the life of Abraham, it was obvious that He greatly reverenced God and was always ready to repent and build an altar of worship and remembrance to God. He built many Altars and all had great significance.

SIGNIFICANCE OF THE ALTARS ABRAHAM BUILT

The first Altar (Genesis: 12) was built to commemorate God's visit and the promise to give Abraham the land of Canaan. Abraham built it to pray and worship and as a reminder of God's promise to bless him. Abraham realized that he could not survive spiritually without regularly renewing his love and loyalty to God. Altars remained in place for years.

The second Altar was **(Genesis 13: 14-15)** after Abraham came back from Egypt where he had lied to Pharaoh about Sarah being his sister and not his wife, and was escorted out in public disgrace; the Lord reappeared to him and renewed the promise. Abraham moved his camp to Hebron where he built an altar and worshipped in a spiritual renewal.

Third Altar was (Genesis: 21:33) after Abraham lied to Abimelech that Sarah was his sister. Abimelech did not know how to trust Abraham afterwards, but respected him because he noticed that God was working with him. He went to Abraham and asked him to swear by God's name that he would not lie to him or his children or grandchildren again. Abraham agreed, signed a treaty, planted a tree in Beersheba and worshipped the Lord.

The Fourth Altar (Genesis: 22:8) At Mt. Moriah following the instruction of God, Abraham built an altar, tied his beloved son Isaac to it and was about to sacrifice him when he was restrained by an angel. A ram caught in the bush was sacrificed instead. He named the place "The Lord will provide".

God tested Abraham, not to trip him and watch him fall but to deepen his capacity to obey God, and to strengthen his character. God refines us through difficulty. When we are tested, we can complain or we can see how God is stretching us to develop our character. In this situation God asked Abraham to perform human sacrifice, something that was forbidden and was done only by pagan nations **(Leviticus 20:1-5).**

God really did not want Isaac to die, but He wanted Abraham to sacrifice Isaac in his heart, so it would be clear that Abraham loved God more than he loved his promised and long-awaited son. Abraham strengthened his commitment and his capacity to obey God and learned about God's ability to provide.

Abraham, the father of faith, along with many others of great faith stature (Hebrews 11) has left us a legacy that cannot be compared. To live a life pleasing to God, we cannot live without faith. **Hebrews 11: 6 says, "But without faith it is impossible to please Him: for he that cometh to God must believe that He is, and that He is a rewarder of them that diligently seek Him.**

Without faith we cannot please God. The rest of the chapter of Hebrews 11 mentions many patriarchs who chose to suffer for their faith than to enjoy the pleasures of this life for a season. Many were beheaded, sawn asunder, suffered with the people of God, had fake trials with angry mockings, and many were stoned to death. Verse 38 of Hebrews says that "**this world was not worthy of them**". They were sold out to God. I aim to be as devoted and sold out to God.

In spite of their dedication to the cause of Christ, verse 39 says "**And these all, having obtained a good report through faith, received not the promise**". It is a heartrending thought to endure such severe hardship without realizing the reward. Yet the scripture says it and the scripture is the word of God.

There is reassurance in knowing that although we may loose in the natural life, we gain in the spiritual in God. Scriptures assure us that we will have to endure hardship in this world, but we are over-comers now and will overcome in the next. "**In the world ye shall have tribulation: but be of good cheer; I have overcome the world**" (John 16:33) KJV.

Here Jesus was reassuring His disciples after telling them about difficulties they would face. If we remember that the ultimate victory has already been won in Christ, we can claim the peace of God in troublesome times.

These mighty Jewish men of God did not receive God's total reward because they died before Christ came. In God's plan they, as well as the Christian believers who were also enduring much testings, will be rewarded together. There is solidarity among believers as reflected in Hebrews 12.

"You have come to Mount Zion, to the city of the living God, the heavenly Jerusalem, and to countless thousands of angels in a joyful gathering. [23] You have come to the Assembly of God's firstborn children, whose names are written in heaven. You have come to God himself, who is the judge over all things. You have come to the spirits of the righteous ones in heaven who have now been made perfect. [24] You have come to Jesus, the one who mediates the new covenant between God and people, and to the sprinkled blood, which speaks of forgiveness instead of crying out for vengeance like the blood of Abel" (Hebrews 12: 22-24) NLT.

God chose to delay their reward but "they saw it from afar". Old and New Testament believers will be glorified together. Not only are we one in the body of Christ with all those alive, but we are also one with all those who ever lived. It takes all of us to be perfect in Him. **"For God had something better in mind for us, so that they would not reach perfection without us" (Hebrews 11:40) NLT.**

Can you identify with Abraham? If so, what part of Abraham's life can you identify with? Can you identify with the courage he displayed throughout his life, leaving security to go to an unknown city and to an unknown God?

Can you see yourself guarding the altar of sacrifice from the vultures all day in the hot sun? Are you maturing in faith and learning from your errors like he did? Even getting to a place where he quit questioning God and took God at His word?

Can you identify with his weakness in compromising his wife by lying that she was his sister, all the time knowing that other men would be vying for her? Can you identify with Abraham as he started the bad habit of lying and later watched as the same thing played out in his son Isaac's life, as he also lied to King Abimelech that his wife Rebecca was his sister?

How about his weakness in passively going along with Sarah's suggestion to sleep with the maid Hagar and impregnate her? Later when there was strife and contention in the house, rather than taking charge and solving the problem, he again listened to Sarah and banished Hagar and her son, Ishmael with a ration of food and water.

How did Abraham get from fear to faith? At what point did the faith seed germinate and spring forth. It seem to have been planted before he left Ur of the Chaldees, his hometown. There he was an idol worshipper. As he journeyed through his uncertain, and many times, problematic life issues we see his strength and weaknesses.

I am sure we all can identify with Abraham, in various aspects and in different degrees. What is heartwarming to me and gives me great hope is the fact that God used Abraham in spite of his flaws. He honored him in such a degree that he was called the "Father of Nations" and the "Father of faith". It gives me great reassurance that God uses the unlikely things to accomplish His work. Here He used a lying idol worshipper to become the father of faith. Paul emphasizes this concept to the Corinthians.

"Remember, dear brothers and sisters, that few of you were wise in the world's eyes or powerful or wealthy when God called you. [27] **Instead, God chose things the world considers foolish in order to shame those who think they are wise. And he chose things that are powerless to shame those who are powerful.** [28]**God chose things despised by the world; things counted as nothing at all, and used them to bring to nothing what the world considers important"** (1Corinthians 1:26-28) NLT.

So Abraham went from fear to faith as he went through a cycle of "messing up" and repenting with a sincere heart. Scriptures say **"If we confess our sins, he is faithful and just to forgive us our sins, and to cleanse us from all unrighteousness"** (1John 1:9) KJV.

With time Abraham became so confident in God that when God asked him to offer up Isaac as a sacrifice, he did not hesitate. His attitude was that God knew best. He also reckoned that God was able to do all things and would raise Isaac from the dead if need be. That's no ordinary faith, but great faith. Remember that Abraham did not have a track record of faith people to follow. He did not know that he had the God of Abraham, God of Isaac, and God of Jacob to depend on. He did not have that experience yet. It was Abraham and the God that he was just learning about. Abraham was the trailblazer of faith. No wonder he was called the Father of Faith. He simply believed God.

"It was by faith that Abraham offered Isaac as a sacrifice when God was testing him. Abraham, who had received God's promises, was ready to sacrifice his only son, Isaac, [18] even though God had told him, "Isaac is the son through whom your descendants will be counted." [19] Abraham reasoned that if Isaac died, God was able to bring him back to life again. And in a sense, Abraham did receive his son back from the dead" (Hebrews 11:17-19).

HOW IS YOUR FAITH?

Take a moment and visit the funeral of Lazarus. Heartbroken and distraught, Martha said to Jesus, **"If you had been here, my brother would not have died" (John 11:21) NIV.** That's called **If only** faith! It says, "if only we lived in the days of Jesus". "If only we could be prayed for by a certain person". "If Only" faith plans for an epitaph, not a resurrection.

When Jesus told Martha that Lazarus would live again she replied**, "I know that he shall rise again in the resurrection" (John 11:24) NIV.** That's called "**Some Day**" faith! People who have it sing "in the sweet by and by." With them everything belongs to the future. But you need to know your rights, your privileges, and your authority – right now. When you do, your life will change radically.

Finally, Martha said, **"But I know that even now God will give you whatever you ask" (John 11:21 NIV).** That is "**even now**" faith! In spite of all you've been through, God has the power to raise you up again. You may have been married and divorced; be struggling with habits; be living in a prison or a penthouse; be black or white, gay or straight; it doesn't matter.

By God's grace and power "even now" you can come out of your grave and live again. All you have to do is open your heart to Jesus today. (From "*A fresh word for today*" Bob Gass).

Chapter 4

✥ Prayer ✥

The simplest definition of prayer is talking to God. Yet that is not all that prayer entails. How about asking of God? How about just being in His presence? How about waiting on God? How about accessing the throne room? God wants His children to abide in Him as referenced in the Book of John 15. We cannot achieve our purpose in this life without abiding in Him.

"I am the true grapevine, and my Father is the gardener. ^{2} He cuts off every branch of mine that doesn't produce fruit, and he prunes the branches that do bear fruit so they will produce even more. ^{3} You have already been pruned and purified by the message I have given you. ^{4} Remain in me, and I will remain in you. For a branch cannot produce fruit if it is severed from the vine, and you cannot be fruitful unless you remain in me." (John 15: 1-3) NLT

Through the means of prayer we abide in God and in abiding in Him we have direct access to His throne room to receive what we need to "rule and reign." His word says **"So let us come boldly to the throne of our gracious God. There we will receive his mercy, and we will find grace to help us when we need it most."**

In <u>Shadows Come to Light</u>, (African Christian Press 2000", Samuel Alfori Onwona said *"Prayer is the avenue God has created for the human race (especially the redeemed of the Lord) to establish His rule and His Kingdom in the affairs of men. Therefore, I see prayer as the most effective means God has given to the Church of the Lord Jesus Christ to enforce Calvary's victory and His rule here on planed Earth."*

In order to rule and reign we have to be in the right position in Christ. Paul said **"[11]Put on the whole armor of God, that ye may be able to stand against the wiles of the devil." (Ephesians 6:11) NLT.** The ensuing scriptures describe how we need to defend ourselves against the enemy. As one reads these words, it becomes clear that most of the armors are essentially passive gifts from the Lord except for the Gospel of Peace and Prayer.

We are required to put on the Helmet of Salvation, the Sword of the Spirit, girded with Truth, Breastplate of Righteousness, and the Shield of Faith. Beyond this the Lord requires us to actively prepare our feet (walk or lifestyle) with the gospel of Peace. Then He said **"[18]Praying always with all prayer and supplication in the Spirit, and watching thereunto with all perseverance and supplication for all saints". (Ephesians 6: 18) KJV**

I agree with Dr Sam in his description, quoted above, of what Prayer really is. Unfortunately we all have come short of praying diligently with perseverance and of praying for all saints. That is why we fail so miserably in making a difference in the world. The scriptures say that **"The earnest prayer of a righteous person has great power and produces wonderful results." (James 5:16) NLT**

- **At the Altar of Prayer God transforms our lives for Ministry**
- **At the Altar of Prayer God prepares us to face trials**

I came upon a wonderful analogy on Prayer. It reads as follows.

The day ended with heavy showers, and the plants in my garden were beaten down by the pelting storm. I looked at one plant I had previously admired for its beauty and had loved for its delicate fragrance. After being exposed to the merciless storm, its flowers had drooped, all its petals were closed, and it appeared that its glory was gone. I thought to myself, "I suppose I will have to wait till next year to see those beautiful flowers again.

Yet the night passed, the sun shone again, and the morning brought strength to my beautiful plant. The light looked at its flowers and the flowers looked at the light. There was contact and communication, and power passed into the flowers. They lifted their heads, opened their petals, regained their glory, and seemed more beautiful than before. I wondered how this took place- these feeble flowers coming into contact with something much stronger, and gaining strength! LB Cowman (Streams in the Desert) Zondervan 1997.

MY OCEAN-LIKE EXPERIENCE AT TRINITY BROADCASTING NETWORK

The Kindergarten experience that I had on my first day of working on the Prayer Line at Trinity Broadcasting Network (TBN) comes to mind. The total experience working at TBN was very rewarding, however my first day I felt like a child looking around for her mother, or some other escape route. Between the time that I washed my hands, signed in, prayed, and sat at my desk, my feet felt like lead.

What made it so daunting for me was the emphasis they had made that "anybody" can be at the other end; in other words I was to expect anything at any time: intimidating questions, profanities, threats, swearing, cursing, just anything, and surely I did experience some of this. Additionally, they emphasized that once I pick the phone up, I could not hang up. The Enemy used the fact that it was a nationally televised program to further intimidate me, so I found it quite daunting.

The Lord has used this "deep-water" experience to groom me into dependency on the Holy Spirit. Human understanding is not astute enough to respond to the deep spiritual needs of people. Our limited view point cannot see into the Spirit. We absolutely have to have the Spirit of God direct us into the things of God. Spiritual discernment sees Spiritual things.

What stands out to me today is how God can transition a person from "fear" (of the flesh) to "faith" (of the Spirit) in a matter of minutes. My sister Sharon was volunteering at the time too, and after sitting there looking at each other being intimidated, we would muster up the courage and begin. Once the "Red" button on the phone was pushed it turned "green" and that notified the operator that we were ready for calls.

When the phone rang we went into prayer taking care of the needs of the people on the other end. Without noticing the transition, we had gone into a ministry that the Holy Spirit Himself had been preparing us for. Everything afterwards flowed as the Spirit led. As I cast the anxieties and cares on Him, He became the wind under my wings, because surely I was buoyed up during those experiences at TBN. God has used this experience and many other intercessory opportunities to strengthen my confidence in prayer.

IS THERE A CORRECT WAY TO PRAY?

As a child I used to say prayers, but now I pray. As a child I repeated prayers that others wrote, but now I pray out of a thankful heart, a cheerful heart, a broken heart, a wounded heart….. In other words I pray out of the sincerity of my own heart. Our merciful Father knows where we are and responds to us accordingly; however He expects us to grow in every aspect of our lives, and for sure, He expects us to grow in prayer.

I am sure the Lord honored my childish prayers then, and accepts every child who comes to Him in prayer now; He accepts even the grown-ups who are at the spiritual maturity level of a child. I used to say this prayer *"gentle Jesus meek and mild, look upon this little child; pity my simplicity….*But I was a child. It is time to put away childish things. The days when I used to pray *"as I lay me down to sleep, I pray the Lord my soul to keep; and if I should die before I wake, I pray the Lord my Soul to take"* are over.

I hasten to make clarification because a person who is in intimate communion with God can just merely groan and it's interpreted by God as very profound. In other words, God is after the true condition of the heart, rather that the content of our words. With wrong motives, the content of our words albeit impressive to the itching ears can reflect a great distance from God.

"Dear brothers and sisters don't be childish in your understanding of these things. Be innocent as babies when it

comes to evil, but be mature in understanding matters of this kind." (1Corinthians 14: 20) NLT

"So let us stop going over the basic teachings about Christ again and again. Let us go on instead and become mature in our understanding. Surely we don't need to start again with the fundamental importance of repenting from evil deeds and placing our faith in God." (Hebrews 6:1) NLT

The Lord makes provisions for His children for every stage of development, and He does expect us to advance to the next stage of maturity. Jesus set a perfect example of how we are to pray. Luke 11 states that He was in a certain place praying and when He was finished His disciples asked Him to teach them to pray. We are in the same boat as the disciples. We need to be taught to pray. *Then* Jesus was with the disciples so He taught them to pray. *Now* the Holy Spirit is with us and He (the Holy Spirit) teaches us to pray.

After Jesus gave the disciples the example of how to pray; honoring His Name, asking for His will on earth, praying for needs, asking for forgiveness, asking for protection against temptation, He then demonstrated how to persist in pray by telling them a story.

PERSISTING IN PRAYER

"Then, teaching them more about prayer, he used this story: "Suppose you went to a friend's house at midnight, wanting to borrow three loaves of bread. You say to him, [6] 'A friend of mine has just arrived for a visit, and I have nothing for him to eat.' [7] And suppose he calls out from his bedroom, 'Don't bother me. The door is locked for the night, and my family and

I are all in bed. I can't help you.' ⁸ But I tell you this—though he won't do it for friendship's sake, if you keep knocking long enough, he will get up and give you whatever you need because of your shameless persistence. "And so I tell you, keep on asking, and you will receive what you ask for. Keep on seeking, and you will find. Keep on knocking, and the door will be opened to you. ¹⁰ For everyone who asks receives. Everyone who seeks finds. And to everyone who knocks, the door will be opened." (Luke 11: 5-10) NLT

Some people believe that if you keep going to God about the same thing over and over, it shows a lack of faith. The aforementioned scripture and many others tell us to persist in prayer. I believe that God enjoys us coming to Him; He wants us to persist in prayer. In fact the struggle we go through in this faith exercise helps to build up our faith. Learn from the story of the widow appealing to the unjust judge.

Parable of the Persistent Widow

¹ "One day Jesus told his disciples a story to show that they should always pray and never give up. ² "There was a judge in a certain city," he said, "who neither feared God nor cared about people. ³ A widow of that city came to him repeatedly, saying, 'Give me justice in this dispute with my enemy.' ⁴ The judge ignored her for a while, but finally he said to himself, 'I don't fear God or care about people, ⁵ but this woman is driving me crazy. I'm going to see that she gets justice, because she is wearing me out with her constant requests!

⁶ Then the Lord said, "Learn a lesson from this unjust judge. ⁷ Even he rendered a just decision in the end. So don't you think God will surely give justice to his chosen people who cry out to

him day and night? Will he keep putting them off? ⁸ I tell you, he will grant justice to them quickly! But when the Son of Man returns, how many will he find on the earth who have faith?" (Luke 18: 1-8) NLT

REASONS TO PRAY

- Pray that you do not be overcome by temptation (Luke 22:40)
- That you will be ministered to by the ministering servants, angels (Luke 22:43)
- Pray that you will be strengthened (Luke 22: 44)
- *Pray to pray* that your prayer will continue –be fervent (Luke22: 46)
- Jesus said "Why are you sleeping? Get up and pray, otherwise temptation will overpower you (Luke 22:46)
- Pray so you do not faint (Luke 18:1)

I am much older now and more mature in my faith. While I do not necessarily see my spiritual progress on a daily basis, every now and then I experience an awakening which shows me that there is advancement in my life. As I aim to put away childish things and focus on a growth walk I am realizing that the Lord wants to deal with me in unusual ways that I do not necessarily like.

Being stretched is not comfortable. I understand also that something that is stretched beyond a certain point will never return to its original position. Like everyone else, I am sure of where I am now; when I am stretched beyond a certain limit I am not sure where I will end up or what I will look like. Does the concept of "fear of the unknown come to mind? Yes! A little trepidation describes my position, but I purpose to trust God. Where I cannot trace His hand I trust His heart.

OTHER INSIGHTS IN PRAYER

The older I get and the more I think I know, the more I realize that there is so much more to know. I pray always for Spiritual discernment because Spiritual things are beyond the natural understanding. Based on my study of God's Word I understand that prayer is the avenue through which we access the resources we need to live a successful life on this side of Eternity.

God made the heavens and the earth and everything else. Then He made man (and woman) in His own image. Initially we had complete access to His throne room and humans were not separated from His presence. But Sin entered and caused a separation. Man had a choice but chose unwisely causing the fall from grace and the separation. With the fall, Satan, the perpetrator gained access to man's rightful position in the Earth (position to rule and reign). Since then Satan has been lording it over man.

Satan is described as the deceiver of the brethren **"And it was not Adam who was deceived by Satan. The woman was deceived, and sin was the result"** (1Timothy 2:13) NLT.

"Even Satan disguises himself as an angel of light" 2Corinthians 11:14) NLT

We see that Satan disguises himself and that he is deceptive. He succeeded in stripping Man of his rightful position to rule and reign on the earth, but God did not leave fallen man in his pitiful position. He made a way.

At the right time God sent His Son Jesus into the world to die for man in order to redeem man back to Himself. He died on the cross, was buried in the grave and was raised on the third day. The scripture further tells us that Jesus went into hell and faced death and the grave and took the sting out of death and said **"I am the living one. I died, but look—I am alive forever and ever! And I hold the keys of death and the grave."** (Revelations 1:18) NLT

So you see! Jesus restored man's original position to rule and reign in this Earth. The original charge still applies – to take dominion over the Earth. **"And God said, Let us make man in our image, after our likeness: and let them have dominion over the fish of the sea, and over the fowl of the air, and over the cattle, and over all the earth, and over every creeping thing that creepeth upon the earth"** (Genesis 1:26) KJV.

"The heaven, even the heavens, are the Lord's: but the earth hath he given to the children of men." Psalm 115: 16) KJV

We can see that God's intention is for us to walk in victory and not in defeat; to be head and not the tail; to be above and not beneath. So why are we living less than victorious lives? Why are we living in defeat?

The Key that Jesus took from the Enemy are not hidden somewhere where we cannot find it. He gave it to Peter and He gave it to every Blood-washed believer. Jesus speaking to Peter, said **"Now I say to you that you are Peter (which means 'rock'), and upon this rock I will build my church, and all the powers of hell will not conquer it. ^{19} And I will give you the keys of the Kingdom of Heaven. Whatever you forbid on earth will be forbidden in heaven, and whatever you permit on earth will be permitted in heaven."** (Matthew 16: 18-19) NLT

This key has been subjected to various interpretations, but either way there is no doubt that it represent authority given by Jesus. Some say it represents the authority to carry out church discipline, legislation and administration (Matthew 18: 15-18); others say the key gives the authority to announce the forgiveness of sins (John 20:23); and still others say the key may be the opportunity to bring people to the Kingdom of Heaven by presenting them with the message of Salvation found in God's Word (Acts 15: 7-9). Regardless of these various interpretations, they all align with God's plan for the believer, to rule, reign and take dominion.

God has great expectation of the Body of Christ, the believers. As He was walking along with His disciples and teaching the people about the Kingdom of God, He told them this: **"He said therefore, a certain nobleman went into a far country to receive for himself a kingdom, and to return. And he called his ten servants, and delivered them ten pounds, and said unto them, Occupy till I come" (Luke 19: 12-14) KJV.**

Jesus is saying the same thing to us. We have to occupy until He comes. Jesus is gone but will return a second time. We have been given excellent resources to build and expand the Kingdom. He expects us to use the gifts and talents that we have been given so that they multiply and the Kingdom grows. He wants each of us to account for what we do with our measure of talent. While waiting for His return, He expects us to rule and reign with the authority that He has given to us and in essence, "Occupy until He comes.

GOD WAITS ON THE BELIEVERS PRAYERS

My understanding about prayer includes the truth that there are some things God will do and there are other things that He expects us to do. He has established the Natural order and He has established the Spiritual order. He gave us a free will and set guidelines in our lives by which we should live. He left us the written Word (The Holy Scriptures), the Holy Spirit, and the Church (the body of believers). We have all the resources that we need to do the work He has left us to do.

In the midst of all the present chaos that is evident around us, do you suppose that God is waiting on the believer's prayers and boldness to access change? After we have put on our spiritual armors to war against the enemy, is there yet more to do? We know that we are in a Spiritual warfare, and so we prepare (Breastplate of Righteousness, Helmet of Salvation, Sword of the Spirit, Belt of Truth, and Preparation by Studying the Word). So, we are dressed and ready for battle, but we need direction from our Commander in Chief (The Holy Spirit).

By what means will we get the directions? How will we hear? If in an army there is no clear channel of communication, then there is chaos. God has left us the means of prayer in order to access His presence to get direction. He said we should not just come, but come boldly and with confidence. **"Let us therefore come boldly unto the throne of grace that we may obtain mercy, and find grace to help in time of need." (Hebrews 4:16) KJV**

After He has done His part, He expects us to do our part. People ask "Why don't we see more miracles?" Well, partly because we are not looking and partly because we are not praying. Miracles still happen every day; but they are reasoned away and the accolades go to the scientists instead of to God.

There are many questions without answers, but if we do more praying and less doubting and depending on our own understanding, we would see more answers to our questions; we would see more answered prayer.

Yes! God is waiting on us to pray. To be in communion with Him, we have to pray. Jesus, the Son of God prayed fervently, constantly and passionately. The Bible says that early in the morning before day, He would go into the mountains to pray. Other places in the Scriptures, tell us that at eventide He would pray.

If Jesus, the sinless Son of God had the need to pray in order to stay close to God and be able to endure, how much more we, sinful man, need to fall on our faces to the King of kings and Lord of lords. He set a perfect example for us to live by and in His Word He said **"And he spake a parable unto them to this end, that men ought always to pray, and not to faint" (Luke 18:1) KJV.**

If we do not pray, we will faint. Many people are fainting instead of accessing our source of strength in God through prayer. God is not going to alter the plan that He has put in place through which we live in Him. He is waiting for us to walk in faith and in obedience.

As Jesus walked along with His disciples, He urged them to pray for workers. Why would Jesus ask the disciples to pray for laborers when He could solve the problem Himself? Because He set His guidelines in place and He would abide with the rules that He and His Father established.

"And Jesus went about all the cities and villages, teaching in their synagogues, and preaching the gospel of the kingdom, and healing every sickness and every disease among the people.

[36]But when he saw the multitudes, he was moved with compassion on them, because they fainted, and were scattered abroad, as sheep having no shepherd.

[37]Then saith he unto his disciples, the harvest truly is plenteous, but the laborers are few;

[38]Pray ye therefore the Lord of the harvest, that he will send forth laborers into his harvest." (Matthew 9: 35-38) KJV

In various places in the scriptures, people are described as sheep and Jesus as the Shepherd. Matthew 9:35-38 is one of those scriptures. Jesus looked at the people following Him and had compassion on them because they were scattered like lost sheep. He saw them also as a full field, ripe and ready for harvest.

Many people around us today are ready to give their lives to Jesus if we would show them how. Jesus commands us to pray for workers to respond to the need of lost souls. He chooses to restrict His power as He waits on His children to respond to His command to pray. He even promised us that we would do greater works than He did when we access Him through prayer.

"I tell you the truth, anyone who believes in me will do the same works I have done, and even greater works, because I am going to be with the Father." (John 14:12) NLT

Often, when we pray for something, God answers our prayers by using us. Be prepared for God to use you to show another person the way to Him. He indeed chooses to wait on our prayers in order to send the laborers, or heal the sick, or provide the means, or save the souls. Again He says **"the harvest truly is plenteous, but the laborers are few; so pray...."**

Discernment through Prayer

Like most people, I have had dreams and plans throughout my life. In trying to live up to what was expected, I jump ahead and worked hard and sometimes fast to achieve. Sometimes I would pray about them, but in essence prayer was basically asking God to bless my plans. When hindrances came up, I would make all effort to circumvent them and continue on the path.

Here I am at a very different place in my life where there is Purpose and a deep desire to walk according to God's plan for my life. Many times, the hindrances that were there blocking my way were there to protect me. The boulders were good for me, only that I did not see it then. I am learning this form James chapter one.

"Dear brothers and sisters, when troubles come your way, consider it an opportunity for great joy. For you know that when your faith is tested, your endurance has a chance to grow" (James 1: 2-3) NLT.

God hedges us in to protect us, but because we see only one side of the hedge, we misunderstand God's actions. Job was in the same predicament as he asked the question. **"Why is light given to a man whose way is hid, and whom God hath hedged in? (Job 3:23) KJV.**

But alas! Satan knew the reason for the hedges for Job and he sure knows them for us. He knows that the purposes of the hedges are not limited to our understanding. For Job, Satan challenged God to remove the hedge from around Job that he (Satan) could have his way with Job. God removed the hedge from around Job reckoning that Job was faithful to God and would endure.

We know the end of the story of Job's life. The scripture puts it this way. **"So the LORD blessed the latter end of Job more than his beginning: for he had fourteen thousand sheep, and six thousand camels, and a thousand yoke of oxen, and a thousand she asses" (Job 42:12) KJV.**

Talking about "putting away childish things"- a child could not understand such things. As I mature in faith walk I understand that in spite of my "mess ups" in life, the Lord has used them for good. I have to put away those tendencies and the way that I have processed life's lessons, and stay focused on God in prayer so that I may discern the way to go. In my devotion yesterday, I read the following from Acts chapter 16.

"[6] Next Paul and Silas traveled through the area of Phrygia and Galatia, because the Holy Spirit had prevented them from preaching the word in the province of Asia at that time. [7] Then coming to the borders of Mysia, they headed north for the province of Bithynia, but again the Spirit of Jesus did not allow them to go there. [8] So instead, they went on through Mysia to the seaport of Troas.

[9] That night Paul had a vision: A man from Macedonia in northern Greece was standing there, pleading with him, "Come over to Macedonia and help us!" [10] So we decided to leave for Macedonia at once, having concluded that God was calling us to preach the Good News there." (Acts 16: 6 -10) NLT

My understanding is that as I pray to God to lead me, I must be looking to see where doors are opening and what doors are closing. I also understand that God will not illuminate the whole journey before us at once, but one step at a time. He desires us to be constantly dependent on Him. God works through the natural order and when He chooses to, He suspends nature and work supernaturally. Many of us are stubbornly looking for the supernatural, even in the face of God patiently beckoning us to see what He is doing in the natural. Paul and the other believers were sensitive to the leading of the Holy Spirit.

We do not know how the Spirit told Paul that he and his companions should not go into Asia. What we know is that they were obedient. To know God's will does not mean we must hear His voice. He leads in different ways. We have to know how God speaks to us individually. When you are seeking God's will;

- Make sure your plans are in harmony with His Word
- Ask mature Christians for their advice
- Check your own motives – are you seeking to do what you want, or what God wants for your life
- Pray for God to open and close the doors as He desires

EFFECTIVE PRAYERS

It is not that some people are super spiritual and can get their prayers answered and others are not. That "super-spiritual" person is simply a person who is disciplined in prayer. The person who prays in faith is not discouraged by unanswered prayer.

Prayer of faith that avails much is prayer that is steadfast and persistent, revived and refreshed, and strengthened by even previous unanswered prayers. As we persist in prayer, the answer is always a little closer; understanding that we are praying with an open heart for the will of God in the prayer request.

Elijah

"Elijah was as human as we are, and yet when he prayed earnestly that no rain would fall, none fell for three and a half years!" (James 5:17) NLT.

There are many other examples of persons who have called on God and are used as great role models for us. Prayers that avail much have to be persistent and earnest. We see great persistence in Elijah's prayer for rain after he had previously prayed and caused drought earlier on in his ministry. Elijah was in constant communion with God, walked in obedience and knew God's plan for the people. Although he knew the plan, he still had to pray and persist in prayer. It took determination and enduring faith. Here is the result of his intercession.

Elijah Prays for Rain

"Then Elijah said to Ahab, "Go get something to eat and drink, for I hear a mighty rainstorm coming!"

[42] So Ahab went to eat and drink. But Elijah climbed to the top of Mount Carmel and bowed low to the ground and prayed with his face between his knees.

[43] Then he said to his servant, "Go and look out toward the sea."

The servant went and looked, then returned to Elijah and said, "I didn't see anything."

Seven times Elijah told him to go and look. ⁴⁴ Finally the seventh time, his servant told him, "I saw a little cloud about the size of a man's hand rising from the sea."

Then Elijah shouted, "Hurry to Ahab and tell him, 'Climb into your chariot and go back home. If you don't hurry, the rain will stop you!'"

⁴⁵ And soon the sky was black with clouds. A heavy wind brought a terrific rainstorm, and Ahab left quickly for Jezreel. ⁴⁶ Then the LORD gave special strength to Elijah. He tucked his cloak into his belt and ran ahead of Ahab's chariot all the way to the entrance of Jezreel." (1 Kings 18: 41-45) NLT

JESUS

Jesus was in great agony and prayed fervently because He knew that the answer was in prayer. **"He prayed more fervently, and he was in such agony of spirit that his sweat fell to the ground like great drops of blood" Luke 22:44) NLT**. Before that Jesus told His disciples to pray that they would not enter into temptation. The Scriptures tell us that as Jesus agonized in prayer and an angel ministered to Him. **"Then an angel from heaven appeared and strengthened him." NLT**

We are called to effectual and fervent prayer that avails much. In other words, we have to grow up and mature in prayer. We have to put away childish prayers and advance in faith and discipline like Elijah did; like Jesus did as He displayed a lifestyle of frequent, passionate prayer on all occasions.

These examples of dedicated prayers warriors show us that there are no exceptions to the prayer discipline that we are called to. There is no special privilege to short-circuit the access route that God has planned. It is established that this is the way to access our resources from God, and that is the means through which He works. Paul addressed the Ephesians, encouraging them to this end.

"Pray in the Spirit at all times and on every occasion. Stay alert and be persistent in your prayers for all believers everywhere." (Ephesians 6:18) NLT

Miracles happen when we prevail in fervent prayer. I have learnt that a miracle is not a suspension of the natural law, but an activation of a higher law. God spoke and the natural law came into being and He said "It is good." He stands by the natural processes that He has put in place. He works through the natural processes, but is not limited to them. He will do whatever He chooses to do on the behalf of His children.

He is the God who rewards faithfulness and many times will even bypass the natural order in order to satisfy and honor His children. He stopped the sun for Joshua and Israel (Joshua 10:13)), He caused the winds and waves to subside for the apostles (Matthew 8), He parted the Red Sea for Israel causing the to walk through the sea on dry ground (Exodus 15). He takes pleasure in working supernaturally for His children; however He has established guidelines by which we must access Him. He said that we should come boldly into His throne room. **"So let us come boldly to the throne of our gracious God. There we will receive his mercy, and we will find grace to help us when we need it most" (Hebrews 4: 16) NLT**

"Prayer does not mean always talking to Him, but sometimes just waiting before him till the dust settles and the stream runs clear" F. B. Meyer. God desires us to be faithful in prayer and He

is the God that rewards faithfulness. His Word assures us how He will miraculously aid us:

"Before the birth pain seven begin, Jerusalem gives birth to a son. Who has ever seen anything as strange as this? Who ever heard of such a thing? Has a nation ever been born in a single day? Has a country ever come forth in a mere moment? But by the time Jerusalem's birth pains begin, her children will be born." (Isaiah 66:7-8) NLT

He loves for us to be in His presence and that is why He chose to have us come through prayer. He gives us our earthly parents as examples. There is no "good" earthly father or mother who would be content if their children would just show up when they need something, then go away without a desire to relate with them.

So is our relationship with our heavenly Father. A mother can be busily doing her chores in the kitchen, and her little boy is on the floor playing contentedly. That mother does not have to be talking nor even engaging her son, neither does the son have to be interacting with his mother. Both are contented in the fact that each is in the others presence, so it is with our Heavenly Father. This contentment is achieved in communion with God through prayer. Obviously prayer is a safe place.

> *"Men may spurn our appeals; they may oppose our arguments; they may despise our sentiments; but they are powerless against our prayers."* Pastor Owen Facey

Chapter 5

✥ Seasons ✥

I believe in and appreciate Seasons. The natural seasons; spring, summer, fall, and winter demonstrate a lot, not just about physical matters, but about Spiritual ones. Seasons tell us about the changes that occur from year to year, and so it is with our personal lives. We change in the different stages of our development.

Sometimes, changes happen so routinely, that we take them for granted, and tend to respond intentionally only to dramatic changes. Consider the natural order of the seasons. Suppose we were to have all winters; then we would have no flowers, no new growth, or birds chirping such as we have during spring and summer. During the fall, there is the beautiful changing of the trees that appeal to the soul in their beauty. At this time nature transitions creation for the stretch of the "barren" winter season when many animals and plants conserve energy by hibernating. Thank God for the changing of the weather and the advent of the seasons.

I believe that the natural, physical things around us all have a Spiritual parallel and so I believe in the Spiritual seasons of my life. I have experienced the changes of the seasons in my life, and if you take time and assess your life, I believe you will attest to the fact that you do have seasonal changes also. Do you notice that sometimes the natural winter season seems unusually long and bitter?

People are snowed in, many loose the natural conveniences such as light and water, and many are house-bound for days or even weeks. During a bad hurricane season many people have their houses "boarded up" for many weeks, if they are fortunate enough to have their houses still standing.

A bad hurricane season can wipe out cities. So it was in South Florida with hurricane Andrew several years ago. That was a season that I will not easily forget. Neither can I forget some of the dark winter seasons of my personal life. As it is in the physical, so it is in the Spiritual.

The spring, summer, and even the fall seasons are relatively pleasant and manageable. The spring is usually crisp, cool, refreshing, warm, beautiful, delightful, inviting, vigorous, bright, and looks prosperous. Then comes the warm summer days, star-lit skies, grass growing, flowers blooming, mosquitoes –biting, kids swimming, baseball playing, fishing, camping, bicycle riding, hot, humid, and rainy; Yes! There are some annoyances too, but mostly manageable.

The fall season rolls along with beautiful golden-brown leaves, the task of raking leaves in the brisk temperature. It is still relatively warm weather. It's a step between summer and winter with some cold days and some warm days. It can be unpredictable, but for the most part it is an enjoyable time of the year with its magnificent colors.

For the purpose of this book I have to set the winter season apart and put special emphasis on it. This is where most people get "stuck" and seem not to readily rebound from. This is the season when the trees are barren, it's cold and many times dreary, there are icy ponds and freezing rivers, dark and foreboding naked trees. Winter can vary between mild and severe, but to be in a severe winter can be a place of isolation and loneliness.

My son and I recently had a discussion and he described an agonizing period of his life as "died and came back to life and died again." I thought he was being melodramatic and said so. He responded that that was his description of his experience. As I thought about it I wondered "who am I to contradict his description of his experience?"

We tend to judge people's situation from a warped perspective based on our own lives. We all have personal agonies. If you do not have any, just hang around a little longer. Sooner or later you will experience a winter spell and you will be looking for words to describe your pain. During this time words are short in coming, or don't come at all. I wonder about people who are unable to express themselves; but thank God for He alone can interpret even the very groans. God speaking to Moses said "**I have certainly seen the oppression of my people in Egypt. I have heard their groans and have come down to rescue them**" (Acts 7:34) NLT.

THE WINTER SEASON

The winter season of the soul is particularly hard. For the most part, people go through isolation and many suffer alone. This is when one experiences the scenario of being in a crowded room, yet feeling lonely. This is when one answers with what people want to hear, rather than saying what they really feel.

Our society has taught us to wear the "acceptable mask", to put on the "respectable smile", and to fake it till you make it. Most of us receive an "A" grade in this class, but unfortunately get no merits toward the Wellness and Wholeness class.

I am at an exciting place in my life where I have come to terms with many unjustifiable things. It's good to come to terms with things that may seem unreasonable or unfair, if not you live in a perpetual state of holding onto offense. I hasten to say that if you hold on to offence which is the root cause of bitterness, resentment, and unforgiveness, then you prolong your winter seasons and delay the more favorable seasons of life. Solomon says this about life.

"For everything there is a season, a time for every activity under heaven. A time to be born and a time to die. A time to plant and a time to harvest. A time to kill and a time to heal. A time to tear down and a time to build up" (Ecclesiastes 3: 1-3) NLT.

Do not prolong your winter season and blight your harvest by holding grudges. Free up yourself to function to the best of your ability in your seasons. You can make wonderful use of your seasons if you accept them for what they are. There is purpose in each of them. God, in His infinite wisdom chose to make these changes a part of our lives on earth.

After the flood, Noah, his children, their families, and all the animals exited the ark. Noah offered up a sacrifice unto God, which God described as a "sweet savor" and God made an oath that He would not smite living creatures as He had done before. Yes! Noah went through his seasons too. God further said in response to Noah's sacrifice, **"As long as the earth remains, there will be planting and harvest, cold and heat, summer and winter, day and night" (Genesis 8:22) NLT.** As it is in the physical so it is in the Spiritual realm. Embrace your seasons. I aim to embrace my seasons as I reflect on the Serenity Prayer.

SERENITY PRAYER

God grant me the serenity
to accept the things I cannot change;
courage to change the things I can;
and wisdom to know the difference. Living one day
at a time;
Enjoying one moment at a time;
Accepting hardships as the pathway to peace;
Taking, as He did, this sinful world
as it is, not as I would have it;
Trusting that He will make all things right
if I surrender to His Will;
That I may be reasonably happy in this life
and supremely happy with Him
Forever in the next.
Amen.

--Reinhold Niebuhr

As I resolve to walk in purpose I am surrendering all my life to God; the good and the bad, the ups and the downs. I have to accept the things that I cannot change and in that I am experiencing an increased capacity to love, to give, and to open up to others. A stark reality hit me recently.

The reality that sometimes, the things we go through are not about us at all, but are about what God wants to accomplish in and through us. This realization propels me further to a place of abandonment in Him. It brings me to a greater acceptance of His purpose for my life.

What do you do during the winter Season? It's in the winter season of our lives that we are best prepared for service. In this season everything has slowed down, and if it is appreciated in the way it is designed to function, energy is conserved. There can be reflection, refreshing, refocusing restoration, rejuvenation and fortitude to face the other seasons when reproduction and advancement take place.

There are great lessons in nature from which we can order our lives. If we study the trees, animals, and the insects, we see a pattern that if we apply to our lives will help us in living successfully. Here is a simplified version of their lives.

The trees sprout new buds and leaves during spring, bear fruit during summer and fall, and shed their leaves and become dormant during the winter. The dormant phase does not mean useless, but it's the phase of greatest conservation of energy in preparation for later production.

The animals and insects live well during spring and summer, gather and store food during the fall, and hibernate during the winter. What lessons can we glean from these speechless parts of creation?

- We are required to produce, so plan ahead. Work during the good times, because the season will change.
- Do not squander all resources, but save for the lean times. **"Take a lesson from the ants, you lazybones. Learn from their ways and become wise! (Proverbs 6:6) NLT.** "Ants—they aren't strong, but they store up food all summer" (Proverbs 30: 25) NLT.
- *"Observe the ants," the great Oriental conqueror Tamerlane told his friends. In relating a story from his early life, he said, "I once was forced to take shelter from my enemies in a dilapidated building, where I sat alone for many hours. Wishing to divert my mind from my hopeless situation, I fixed my eyes on an ant carrying a kernel of corn larger than itself up a tall high wall. I counted its attempts to accomplish its feat. The corn fell sixty nine times to the ground, but the insect* **persevered**. *The seventieth time it reached the top. The ant's accomplishment gave me courage for the moment, and I never forgot the lesson." From the King's Business.* (Stream in the Desert) L.B. Cowman
- As the trees shed their leaves during the fall in order to preserve energy, shed the unnecessary collection of "stuff" that are really purposeless. Sometimes we have to shed even some relationships.
- Do not fight against the changing of the seasons, just accept and prepare for it. Accept it as a part of your journey, just as you accept the physical cold winter season. Acceptance brings release and relief.
- Winter season of loneliness and isolation is necessary for soul-searching, rejuvenation, and refreshing.

- It has been well documented that many have come to a bigger and better place after a period of isolation (winter experience).

Abraham was "alone in the land of Canaan, while Lot lived among the cities" (Genesis 13:12), Moses spent 40 years alone in the dessert with God, and Paul, after spending time "at the feet of Gamaliel" (Acts 22:3) was required after meeting Jesus, to go "immediately into Arabia" (Galatians 1: 7) to learn of the dessert (winter experience) life with God. You have to be alone with God to learn from Him.

Jacob was alone as he wrestled with the angel of God (Genesis 32:28) and he got the blessing. Daniel was alone when he had his heavenly visions, and John was banished on the Isles of Patmos, when he got the Revelations of Jesus (Revelations 1:1). My beloved friends, although the natural mind cannot readily welcome the winter season, accept it anyway, because it is vitally necessary for the Soul and the Spirit. Remember that you are never really alone, because the Father is with you during the drought experience. **"I am not alone because the Father is with me" (John 16:32) NLT**

CURRENT HARD KNOCKS

Having gone around the block a few times in my life so far, and having experienced the changes of the seasons in many ways, I have a better understanding of life. There is still much to understand but I can appreciate the changes. There are some things I understand by observing other people's lives, but other things I have had to experience myself in order to get a deeper impact; I believe it may be so with you also.

I hope that writing about my experiences and showing how I came through, will encourage a sister, a mother, a friend, a neighbor, and anyone who can identify with such concerns, to live a life according to their God given purpose and not live less than they are meant to live. If there are no clear guidelines and boundaries in your lives, you can shift your position so often and so subtly that you are not readily aware of the change.

Just like it's possible to put a frog in cold water and set it on a hot stove, and that frog acclimatizes to the change of temperature so that it gets cooked, so it's possible that you can lose yourselves in compromise.

I do a lot of reflecting when I drive, and in one of my recent reflective moments a few days ago, I smiled and said to myself "It is good that I have gone through." I remembered the quote from Paul's epistle to the Romans. **"We can rejoice, too, when we run into problems and trials, for we know that they help us develop endurance. And endurance develops strength of character, and character strengthens our confident hope of salvation"** (Romans 5: 3-4) NLT.

James, in writing to the Jewish believers also encouraged them to see trial as opportunity to endure and to advance in the things of God. **"Dear brothers and sisters, when troubles come your way, consider it an opportunity for great joy. For you know that when your faith is tested, your endurance has a chance to grow. So let it grow, for when your endurance is fully developed, you will be perfect and complete, needing nothing"** (James1:2-4)NLT

Here I am at another winter season of my life. This "oak tree" is learning to bend to the winds of life that assail her. I am facing another divorce and dealing with it as an opportunity for grace extended and received. There is always a choice for us of walking in bitterness and resentment, or walking in love and forgiveness. I choose to walk in forgiveness, so I give my pain and disappointment to God as frequently as I am aware of them.

On my own I would easily hold on to bitterness and resentment, but with God it is possible to love when the natural mind says to "hate". Needless to say I am disappointed for the turn of my life, however I have strong confidence that this phase is a stepping stone to a better stage.

Some may think that my reason for writing this part of my life is to be scandalous; I beg to disagree, in fact I would be scandalizing myself too. My mode of functioning has been to cover rather than expose, so much so that I have felt "foolish" in my effort to cover issues many times. My aim is not to malign in any way, but to encourage others.

I believe that my brokenness in relationships has taught me compassion and sensitivity to hurting people. I also believe that there is an element of purpose in this brokenness that has nothing to do with me or my husband. God uses the broken pieces of our lives to accomplish His purpose, even to minister to those who we do not even know.

In the beginning of our marriage, my husband and I talked about our desire for God to use us as a unit to minister to married couples. As our marriage fell apart, I reminded the Lord of our prayer. Things got worse instead of better, as there was a head-strong wind that kept blowing pride, arrogance, stubbornness, offence, blame and unforgiveness. All this has brought us to a place that demands a courageous decision. Are we committing to our marriage or getting out of it.

As I deleted three paragraphs of my story, I acknowledge that I am at a very difficult juncture in my writing. I keep erasing, rewriting, and erasing again; so I walked away. This is the place where wisdom is of paramount importance. I am aware that there is only a very thin line between being transparent and being unwise. What would be without merit and actually detract from the essence and purpose of this book would be for me to detail negative stories and neglect to emphasize the positive outcomes. Undoubtedly there have been struggles but I can say with great confidence that the difficulties have brought me to a bigger and better place.

The Lord has challenged me to be courageous. Writing all this is taking a great deal of courage. My natural tendency is to do the easy thing; don't ruffle the feathers; don't rock the boat and just float downstream rather that swim against the current.

But I sense that my writing is important at this time. I have to do the unpopular thing. Reflecting on how we desired our marriage to be an example yet it is in a state of demise, I cannot help but wonder WHY. Some answers have come to me and this one has stood out.

- God will not force our hearts; we have to be willing.

Even in the middle of a divorce, the Lord is reassuring me that all is not lost and that there is still purpose in this. My limited mind has been focusing on what generally marriage means to most of us, but in God's economy the bottom line is discovering and following His direction.

I just trust Him as I go along because I know that only God can make a way out of no-way; only my God can bring life out of death, so I do what He directs me to do and leave the rest to Him. God has reminded me of the scripture where the priest Samuel's was weeping over King Saul whom God had rejected as king of Israel because of his disobedience. **"And the LORD said unto Samuel, How long wilt thou mourn for Saul, seeing I have rejected him from reigning over Israel?"(1 Samuel 16:1) KJV.**

I realized that I had to move on with my life and stop weeping over a marriage that has been dead. Our lives can become complicated and crooked by our own doing – such as walking in disobedience, or it can be crooked in spite of our good efforts. Either way, taken in the right perspective, it can be "turned for good". I am accepting the things that I cannot change.

"Accept the way God does things, for who can straighten what he has made crooked"? (Ecclesiastes 7:13) NLT.

God allows the crookedness of our lives to be the platform from which to display His might and Power. I still believe that God is able to make something beautiful of my life, my husband's life and your life, if we are willing. No one is beyond help and the challenges are designed to effect change in us and those around us. The one who has never been in a battle would not know how to prepare a soldier.

Could it be that the person who can speak with authority on positive and successful relationships is the one who has been through brokenness in relationships? God has called me to be an Encourager. I have wondered if it was possible to encourage others without having been tainted with the wounds, pains, and scars that wounded people experience. How can one encourage others, if such a person has not been in need of encouragement, received encouragement, and know the difference it makes. We are all still works in progress.

I remember playing doll house as a little girl. Then, I was always the mother comforting the children. I remember as a young woman how I was usually the peacemaker trying to make things right and seeing that everyone was well. I am not portraying myself as a perfect person because I have had my own share of wrong-doings in life, but what I am proposing is that God prepares His people in various ways to do His purpose and He has prepared me.

I understand that His hands were molding me from the. My preparation as a Registered Nurse further equips me in the area of care giving and nurturing that hurting people need. With all that said, the insight that I have gotten into my true purpose causes me to look back and see that He was there all the time weaving the fabric of my life together.

The wounds and battle scars are being used also. I conclude that it is necessary to be bruised to know what a bruise feels like. If you have not been in the dark tunnels, you could not identify with the fright experienced by the person going through. If you've never been in a storm, you would not know what hard winds feel like. And again, if you've not been in a battle, you would not be able to prepare a soldier for war.

It is good that I've been through, so that I can help others going through. There are many who have been through "tough times" and choose to stand back; but the word for you is to let those tough times be your stimulus to be an encourager.

The difficulties that I have had in my relationships have humbled me. It is a good place to be as I now realize that my expectations were misplaced. I now have "far less" expectation of man, but great expectations of God. I totally depend on Him. I have need encouragement, received it, and I am in a position to emphasize with those who weep.

CHAPTER 6

❧ LIFE ~ A PARADOX? ❧

In contemplating the issues of life, would you say that life is a paradox? There are so many apparent contradictions in life that many times, one is left in a quandary as to how it will work out. A scripture passage that has kept me focused, centered, and grounded goes as follows, **"For I know the plans I have for you," says the LORD. "They are plans for good and not for disaster, to give you a future and a hope. (Jeremiah 29:11) NLT.**

The Amplified version of the Bible describes it **as** God giving me "hope in my final outcome." I have concluded that regardless of all the unanswered questions, the contemplations, the puzzles, the disappointments, the things that do not add up, God has a plan to take me to an expected end.

Solomon contemplated life and its apparent contradictions. He made many paradoxical statements that leave us searching for answers, yet the answers are there and are truly profound.

"Sorrow is better than laughter, for sadness has a refining influence on us" (Ecclesiastes 7:3) NLT

For sure sorrow is God's way of tilling the soil of our souls to produce a greater harvest. Sorrow causes us to think deeply and seriously about the issues of life. Laughter is a more light and superficial emotion that, although necessary does not get to the depth of the Soul. Another sobering quote from Solomon says;
"A wise person thinks a lot about death, while a fool thinks only about having a good time" (Ecclesiastes 7:4) NLT

Solomon is not encouraging us to think morbidly about death, but to think clearly and to take into account the direction of our lives. Because everyone will eventually die we are admonished to consider that fact and to make the necessary preparation to experience God's mercy instead of His justice.

I remember in the past, making hasty statements like "I would never do this or I would never do that." Over the years I have had many "curve balls" thrown at me that resulted in me acting out of character, I now conclude that I cannot dictate or direct my life.

I understand that I am always responsible for my actions regardless of the cause and that my dependency is upon God to enable me to walk after the Spirit and not after the flesh. In the midst of all the apparent contradictions of life, I choose to trust the God who made me.

"Trust in the LORD with all your heart and lean not on your own understanding; in all your ways acknowledge him ,and he will direct your paths." (Proverbs 3, 5-6)

Growing up, I heard my mother with this statement on many occasions.

"Pig did ask im mame whe mek im mout so long?"

The response "A come yu a come, yu wi find out."

Interpretation: The pig asked his mother "why is your mouth so long?" The mother responded, "You are growing, you will find out".

Surely as I grew up I understood the depth of that statement. There are many things that we will never understanding until we have experienced them for ourselves. Rather than complaining about them, we need to take the attitude of Paul in his letter to the Romans;

"We can rejoice, too, when we run into problems and trials, for we know that they help us develop endurance. And endurance develops strength of character, and character strengthens our confident hope of salvation. And this hope will not lead to disappointment. For we know how dearly God loves us, because he has given us the Holy Spirit to fill our hearts with his love" (Romans 5:3-5) NLT.

At this juncture of my life, I am humbled as I continue my faith journey. I used to have certain expectations based on how circumstances stacked up. I used to have definite understanding of cause and effect. I used to be, and still am that person who like to see all the ducks in a row. Well! Life has shown me in no uncertain terms that there is no guarantee in this natural life. The only thing that I am sure of is my Salvation in Jesus Christ.

It's tough when you expend all your energies on a project and it fails. It's very disappointing when you study and prepare yourself for an exam, and fail the test. It's very concerning when you eat healthily, yet end up with a heart attack or some other unexpected disease.

Years ago, I met a patient who was very angry because she jogged everyday, ate all the right foods and thought she was in tip top shape. She was admitted to the hospital for a heart attack. While she talked, I felt her emotional and mental pain, as she described how she had sacrificed a lot to maintain her "good" health. I am sure that many of you can attest to the fact that many scenarios in your lives are puzzling and tantamount to just downright contradictory.

Solomon, the wisest man who ever lived, found life puzzling. In his writing in Ecclesiastes, he started out describing everything as meaningless.

"Everything is meaningless," says the Teacher, "completely meaningless!" (Ecclesiastes 1:2) NLT.

He came to this conclusion as he contemplated the monotony of all that was around him, the routine work of man, and the dissatisfaction of humans. Solomon concluded after much deliberation and soul searching that there is purpose and a duty for us in life.

"**Here now is my final conclusion: Fear God and obey his commands, for this is everyone's duty.** [14] **God will judge us for everything we do, including every secret thing, whether good or bad**" (Ecclesiastes 12: 13-14) NLT.

PREVIOUS CONCEPTS OF MARRIAGE

Because I am sure of my foundation in Christ, I too conclude that my purpose is to serve Him. As a young woman growing up, I used to have a very idealistic approach to marriage and an insensitive approach to divorcees. In fact I was idealistic in almost every aspect of life. I was naïve and unrealistic.

Now I realize that I had ideal standards in the areas that I was strong in, and that I actually played down my weak areas. Isn't that the general behavior of most of us? We tend to be very judgmental of others who do not measure up to our self-determined "framework" for their lives; and we become judge and jury in the areas of their weakness.

That was how I felt about divorcees. I had very strong beliefs in people staying together in marriage, regardless of the reasons. I naively thought that it was always workable, not considering that both parties have to be "walking together" to make a relationship work. I thought that adultery was the only exception to the rule and that all other reasons were "trite". This judgmental attitude towards divorcees was so intense that I would not have a friend that was divorced. I would keep them at a far distance. I was insensitive and downright prejudiced.

I have since then wondered why I felt so strongly about marriage and divorce. Was it because I was self-righteous? Was it because I inappropriately took on offense and walked in this offense, instead of walking in forgiveness? Was it due to ignorance? Could it be that because I had not been tainted with divorce YET, that pride took me in a direction of setting up this lofty standard that most, including myself, could not attain? Whatever the real reason, or combination of reasons, I know that it was not charitable. I was very insensitive to the pain and suffering of people in this need.

THE PARADIGM SHIFT

It is unfortunate that at times we have to go through deep personal pain to come out on the other side with a new mindset. My understanding now is that we are all flawed in all areas of our lives and have the propensity of acting out of our deepest pain. In acting out against others, we have a subconscious agenda of making ourselves look and feel better. We continue in this mind-set unless we come into a face to face contact with God, who reveals truth to us and grant us mercy for others.

Having gone through a very painful divorce, and now experiencing another difficult relationship, I realize that there are times when you could do everything within your power and still come up lacking in relationship.

I believe that God is using these failed relationships to peel off layers of pride and insensitivity. As I am being sustained in the middle of my trying times, I realize that He is using the dysfunctional situation as an asset to propel me to a higher Spiritual level in Him. Many times God uses the adversities and the adversary (Satan) – the One who many times perpetuate the chaos in our lives, to our advancement and his ultimate demise.

Over time and experiences, I have come to a new appreciation of marriage, the perplexing issues that can be involved in it and more of the variables and grey areas that can force a divorce. Some may say that my change of heart is just to cover my own failures or that now I am compromising, or any other reason you may come up with. I positively know that God hates Divorce and desires that people should live in peace.

"Never pay back evil with more evil. Do things in such a way that everyone can see you are honorable. Do all that you can to live in peace with everyone. Dear friends, never take revenge. Leave that to the righteous anger of God. For the Scriptures say, "I will take revenge; I will pay them back," says the LORD (Romans 12: 17-19) NLT.

Jesus also pointed out that Moses allowed a divorce decree because of the hardness of people's hearts. People would rather keep offending rather that keep forgiving. I understand that God's original plan is that we live in peace. In His response to the Pharisees enquiring about divorce Jesus said:

"Since they are no longer two but one, let no one split apart what God has joined together." "Then why did Moses say in the law that a man could give his wife a written notice of divorce and send her away?" they asked. Jesus replied, "Moses permitted divorce only as a concession to your hard hearts, but it was not what God had originally intended" (Matthew 19: 6 - 8) NLT.

It was very painful going through an abusive marriage several years ago. Because of the lofty expectations that I had set for myself and my hate for divorce, I stuck to my conviction to maintain the marriage at all cost. It took being hit unconscious and getting a glimpse of a possible "murder charge" for me to wake up to a new understanding; A new understanding that the relationship that I was in was no longer a marriage and that the harshness and abuse was really what God hated. I understood that getting out of that abuse was not displeasing to God.

That was a defining moment in my life when I knew that my body, the temple of the Holy Spirit, should be honored and treated with respect. You will not see it worded in the Bible "Thou shalt not abuse thy spouse", but the intent is all over the Scriptures;

"As the church submits to Christ, so you wives should submit to your husbands in everything.

For husbands, this means love your wives, just as Christ loved the church. He gave up his life for her [26] **to make her holy and clean, washed by the cleansing of God's word"** (Ephesians 5: 24-26) NLT.

"In the same way, husbands ought to love their wives as they love their own bodies. For a man who loves his wife actually shows love for himself" (Ephesians 5: 28) NLT.

"Husbands, love your wives and never treat them harshly" (Colossians 3:9) NLT.

Many people of God have been subjected to a warped understanding of Christianity. Many have come under legalism of do's and don'ts, rather than living in love and forgiveness. We have heard over and over again "wives, submit to your husbands" till "death do you part" yet "husbands love your wives" or the verse that admonish us to submit to one another get left unsaid. Many times, "till death do you part" is really what happens, when all along the perpetrator gets acclaimed while the victim gets ignored.

There are many Scripture that exhort us to walk in liberty and freedom. Christ teaches us not to be entangled in bondage. **"Stand fast therefore in the liberty wherewith Christ hath made us free, and be not entangled again with the yoke of bondage"** (Galatians 5:1) KJV.

In spite of these teachings, many of us walk about like victims. We are in bondage because of fear of other's opinions, fear of being ostracized by groups and even the Church, and many are even enslaved by warped interpretation of Scriptures.

But in Christ, we are free and the Holy Spirit is available to teach us how to live in freedom.

"If the Son therefore shall make you free, ye shall be free indeed" (John 8:36) KJV.

"Now we have received, not the spirit of the world, but the spirit which is of God; that we might know the things that are freely given to us of God. Which things also we speak, not in the words which man's wisdom teacheth, but which the Holy Ghost teacheth; comparing spiritual things with spiritual" (1Corinthians 2:12-13) KJV.

If you know the Lord, and if you walk in relationship with Him daily, He will speak to you uniquely regarding your unique situation; withstanding that His "Rhema Word" always line up with His "Logos Word." A (Rhema) Word is "a Word from the Word" referring to the revelation received by the reader from the Holy Spirit when the (Logos) Word is read. **"The Comforter, which is the Holy Ghost, whom the Father will send in my name, he shall teach you all things, and bring all things to your remembrance, whatsoever I have said unto you"** (John 14:26) KJV.

COURAGE

There are many reasons, including lack of knowledge of the Word and lack of courage to act, that the Kingdom of God continues to suffer violence. **"And from the days of John the Baptist until now the kingdom of heaven suffereth violence, and the violent take it by force"** (Matthew 11:12) KJV.

There are three common views suggesting the meaning of this Scripture.

- Jesus may have been referring to a vast movement towards God, the momentum that began with John's preaching.
- Jesus may have been reflecting the Jewish activist's expectation that God's Kingdom would come through a violent overthrow of Rome.
- Jesus may have meant that entering God's Kingdom takes courage, unwavering faith, determination, and endurance because of the growing opposition leveled at Jesus followers.

Regardless of your take on this Scripture, it is clear that living in the Kingdom of God is not a life of ease and lack of challenges, but rather frequent turbulent and forceful windstorms that have to be combated. A broken relationship is an area where the Kingdom of God constantly suffers great violence.

Whether in marriage, in sibling relationship, or parent-child relationship...when you are caught up in a dysfunctional relationship, if you do not know your true value and purpose you can be swept away in the currents of the woes. If you know who you are in Christ and know what He has called you to be and to do, then nothing – including that dysfunctional situation should keep you from your calling.

"What sorrow awaits the world, because it tempts people to sin. Temptations are inevitable, but what sorrow awaits the person who does the tempting. So if your hand or foot causes you to sin, cut it off and throw it away. It's better to enter eternal life with only one hand or one foot than to be thrown

into eternal fire with both of your hands and feet. And if your eye causes you to sin, gouge it out and throw it away. It's better to enter eternal life with only one eye than to have two eyes and be thrown into the fire of hell" (Matthew 18: 7-9) NLT.

Gigi Graham Tchividjian wrote *"I stood in the doorway, watching my son walk slowly down the driveway and out into the street. Then, with a heart that felt heavy as lead, I reluctantly turned away."*

She had made all the efforts that a loving mother could make for her son, and had watched him rebelled, spurned the efforts of the family, and disdained the family values under which he was raised. She further wrote, *"I had never expected to be awakened late at night by police officers holding large dogs on tight leashes at the front door, calls from detention centers, unsavory friends, drugs, theft, and wild dress to go with even wilder behavior. Why? Our other children, although not perfect, had never caused us any serious problems.*

Unable to control tears, I thought about all the chances we had given our son. He had run away from home at sixteen. We had taken him back again and again only to have him abuse our trust and disrupt our family life. We had done all we knew to do until finally, tonight, my husband had to demand that he leave our home." (Prodigals and those who love them) Ruth Bell Graham Baker Books 2009.

In this life there are no guarantees. Things don't necessarily work out the way we expect them to and in fact many times go contrary to all you positive efforts. Typically prodigals refer to wayward children, but practically there are many wayward wives, husbands, parents, children...As the one who have a prodigal, there comes a time that you have to allow the prodigal to go in order to safeguard the homestead. Always leave an open channel of communication and be willing to forgive. Then it's up to the prodigal to come to his or her senses and seize the opportunity to return.

God is love and He has called us to love and to forgive. No one should be hated, abused, or victimized by another. The whole essence of the gospel of Christ is to love and to forgive. Applying this to marriage, how can we say we love and find it so hard to forgive? But is a struggle if you have forgiven and forgiven and forgiven again.

I smile as I remember a part in a musical where the man asked Jesus how many times he should forgive his brother and Jesus replied "Forgive until you lose all count of counting, then forgiveness will be a part of you."

God has given each person a measure of endurance and He wants us to work out the issues of our lives with wisdom to the best of our ability. Paul encouraged the Philippians to honor Christ in their lives by living as he guided them. We must aim to represent Christ to the best of our ability; in doing so we live with a clear conscience pleasing God, rather than trying to please man who we can never please.

"Dear friends, you always followed my instructions when I was with you. And now that I am away, it is even more important. Work hard to show the results of your salvation, obeying God with deep reverence and fear" (Philippians 2:12) NLT.

"If you need wisdom, ask our generous God, and he will give it to you. He will not rebuke you for asking" (James 1:5) NLT.

God expects us to use wisdom in our dealings with each other. If you are walking with God and are in tune with His leading, you will understand when "enough is enough" in each situation. God will show you the way out. You will miss the promptings if you are not walking with Him.

It behooves us all to know the Word of God, be in tune with the Holy Spirit, and maintain a personal relationship with Him. If you do not do this, then you will always be depending on somebody else's interpretation of what God is saying. God desires to relate with each of us.

I came to that place for myself. I know and am still learning the Word and I am more in tune with the Holy Spirit through prayer. I surround myself with praying prayer partners and I have a Spiritual Mentor. I am still a work in progress, but God has certainly brought me from a place of uncertainty to a better place of confidence in Him.

After surviving the abusive marriage, it took over twenty years before I could muster up confidence in allowing myself into a relationship again. God has healed me of heartache and deep disappointments. I believe that my second marriage twenty five years later, helped to restore my confidence.

I have seen many bitter women and men too, who have been completely turned off of relationships and if they are in one, they are in it for the wrong reasons. I thank God that I have released offence and that it did not turn into resentment and bitterness. I know that there are many "good" men out there; men who honor their wives and their homes; ones who are faithful and lead with integrity; ones who work diligently to provide for their families; and those who lead their families into Spiritual truths. Thank God for men who are good examples.

My husband and I have been married for 7½ years; years of natural ups and downs, like most marriages. What I realized quite early in the marriage was that the marriage was being drained of emotional reserve that was not being replenished. We were not working together in restoring and sustaining the marriage.

We were not creating new memories for our relationship and after a while there was nothing to sustain. Another issue was unresolved conflicts. My husband was desperately fearful of conflicts; and of course conflicts come whether you want them or not. He specialized in avoiding, at all cost, the opportunities to resolve them. Is it a wonder that they did not go away by themselves? Well! They did not.

Beyond my husband, I trusted God from the very beginning. I believed then, and still believe that there was purpose in our getting together. We got the opportunity to represent God in our lives together as a couple, but sadly it was derailed by lack of cooperation, stubbornness, unforgiveness and deception. As I experienced disconnect and continued indifference in the marriage I have had some hard questions without clear and definitive answers.

DO I HAVE TO BE HUMILIATED TO BE HUMBLE?

I would quickly answer "No" to this question. My husband has a passion for doing things for people. Unfortunately he doesn't set boundaries and many times the home was compromised; so I would ask this question in my mind. Time and time again, I had to ask myself the question. One day I asked my wise and faithful mentor "Do I have to be humiliated to be humble?" It seemed like I was being processed.

I got an answer from my mentor that not only clarify some things for me, but gave me great reassurance that there was a purpose for the journey that I was on.

She said; "Humiliation is of the Flesh, but Humility is of the Spirit". She further explained that sometimes you have to work through Humiliation to get to Humility.

As I write this I am remembering when I had a vision of a banana being peeled and the interpretation came to me that I was that banana. The Holy Spirit told me that He would peel layers off of me. I remember also how Jesus was humiliated by men; how He was spat upon; how He was beaten; how He endured shame and disgrace at the hands of sinful man, for my sake. So I receive that wise explanation with humility.

WOULD GOD DIRECT A DIVORCE?

It is established that God hates Divorce. This is what tugs at the heart of a believer when faced with the possibility of a divorce. In this "tight" place you have to know the voice of God and have to know the Word. This is where a personal relationship with God is critical. God deals with us uniquely and He knows the intricacies of each life.

As I struggled with the unpopular decision, I dug deep and stayed steadfast at the feet of Jesus to get my answer. Little by little the Lord revealed some things to me.

- He showed me a vision of a PIE and the different segments of the PIE. I saw the segment that represented the marriage and then He said never to let any part of that PIE overshadow the whole. No segment of my life should overtake my whole life. The next time I saw the

PIE, the segment represent representing the marriage was shriveled like a prune.

- Over a year or so, I have been very expectant and excited with anticipation to see God work in my life. In spite of the recent difficulties in my life including surgery and chemo, God has given me a great gift of joy in spite of pain and disappointments. As I kept coming to God about my marriage, telling Him that He is who I am looking to for changes, I was surprised and disappointed when I eventually got clear a denial from Him. When I asked Him to work it out, He said "No, I will not." The Lord then impressed on my heart that there are some things He will do and other things we, as His people, have to do. He has waited patiently for my husband and I to comply with His guidelines for a successful marriage, but we would not. He further released me with the Scripture;

"What sorrow awaits the world, because it tempts people to sin. Temptations are inevitable, but what sorrow awaits the person who does the tempting. So if your hand or foot causes you to sin, cut it off and throw it away. It's better to enter eternal life with only one hand or one foot than to be thrown into eternal fire with both of your hands and feet. And if your eye causes you to sin, gouge it out and throw it away. It's better to enter eternal life with only one eye than to have two eyes and be thrown into the fire of hell" (Matthew 18: 7-9) NLT.

WOULD GOD JUST SIT BACK AND NOT ACT ON HIS CHILDREN'S BEHALF?

I have waited and waited, and expected Him to turn thing around in our marriage. I have done my part and expected Him to do His part, (*as if He has not done so much for us daily*). I have taken comfort in this Scripture as I waited. **"The king's heart is like a stream of water directed by the LORD; He guides it wherever he pleases" (Proverbs 21:1) NLT.**

With this I was expecting God to take a hold of my husband's heart. I'll tell you that I put my heart up in front of Him daily also; in any case I expected change.

Recently I got a new appreciation of what this Scripture really means and it reinforces my understanding that many times God holds back because of the "free will" principle that He has implemented in our lives, where He allows us to choose. He will not go contrary to His plan.

And how does God deal with the stubborn will? Especially when that will is the object of loving, concerned, even desperate prayer? Matthew Henry writes *"God can change men's minds, can turn them from that which they seemed most intent upon, as the husbandman, by canals and gutters, turns the water through his ground; which does not alter the nature of the water, not put any force upon it; any more than God's providence does upon the native freedom of man's will, but directs the course of it to serve His own purpose."* (Prodigals and those who love them) Ruth Bell Graham Baker Books 2009.

WOULD GOD ALLOW HIS PEOPLE TO SIN?

The reality of the answer to this question hit me straight between the eyes. "Yes"! God will allow His people to sin because of the choice that He has given to them. He shows us good and evil and challenges us to choose. He spoke through Joshua to His people, challenging them to make a choice; so Joshua said:

"So fear the LORD and serve him wholeheartedly. Put away forever the idols your ancestors worshiped when they lived beyond the Euphrates River and in Egypt. Serve the LORD alone. But if you refuse to serve the LORD, then choose today whom you will serve. Would you prefer the gods your ancestors served beyond the Euphrates? Or will it be the gods of the Amorites in whose land you now live? But as for me and my family, we will serve the LORD." The people replied, "We would never abandon the LORD and serve other gods" (Joshua 24: 14-16) NLT.

If you walk in rebellion and disobedience, God will allow you to fall and face the consequences. There are many of our forefathers who have suffered and paid the consequences and we are experiencing the same today. Moses had to face harsh punishment from God because of disobedience.

"Then he and Aaron summoned the people to come and gather at the rock. "Listen, you rebels!" he shouted. "Must we bring you water from this rock?" [11] Then Moses raised his hand and struck the rock twice with the staff, and water gushed out. So the entire community and their livestock drank their fill.

But the LORD said to Moses and Aaron, "Because you did not trust me enough to demonstrate my holiness to the people of Israel, you will not lead them into the land I am giving them!" (Numbers 20: 10-12) NLT

The Lord had told Moses to speak to the Rock; however Moses struck it, not once but twice. God did the miracle; yet Moses was taking credit for it when he said of him and Aaron, "must we bring water from the rock?" For this he was forbidden to enter the Promised Land. Was God's punishment to Moses too harsh?

After all, the people had nagged him, slandered him, and rebelled against both him and God. Now they were at it again (Numbers 20:5). But Moses was the leader and model for the entire Nation. Because of this great responsibility to the people, he could not be let off lightly. By striking the Rock, Moses disobeyed God's direct command and dishonored God in the presence of His people.

David also went out of alignment with God's will when he took a census of his army.

"Satan rose up against Israel and caused David to take a census of the people of Israel. [2] So David said to Joab and the commanders of the army, "Take a census of all the people of Israel—from Beersheba in the south to Dan in the north—and bring me a report so I may know how many there are."

But Joab replied, "May the LORD increase the number of his people a hundred times over! But why, my lord the king, do you want to do this? Are they not all your servants? Why must you cause Israel to sin?" But the king insisted that they take

the census, so Joab traveled throughout all Israel to count the people" (1Chronicles 21: 1-4) NLT

David's census taking brought disaster to Israel, not so much so that the census was wrong, but more so that his motive was wrong. God was taking pride in his military strength rather than in depending on God as he had done before. There is a thin line between feeling confident because you are relying on God's power and becoming proud because have been used by God to do great work.

The Bible said that Satan caused David to take a census. Can Satan force people to do wrong? "No"! Satan only tempted David with the idea, but David decided to act on the temptation. Ever since the Garden of Eden, Satan has been tempting people to Sin, but we have a God-given choice not to yield.

God provided David an "out clause" in the Joab's council, but David's curiosity was spurred on by arrogance, and he exercised faith in his own strength rather than in God. David, like Moses, had to face the consequences of his wrong decision. Unfortunately many innocent lives were lost because of his disobedience.

"So the LORD sent a plague upon Israel, and 70,000 people died as a result" (1Chronicles 21:14) NLT.

I understand that there are consequences to our behavior and that God will allow us to fail in order to teach us and bring us to a higher level in Him. I believe that in the middle of my broken marriage is the potential for restoration and Spiritual advancement, if there is willingness to do what it takes to nurture and maintain a relationship.

If God would step in and do for us what He has already instructed us to do, but we are unwilling, then God would be negating His own principle of choice. He has given to us a free will. If we sit in complacency, or choose disobedience, arrogance, stubbornness, or rebellion instead of humility, love and forgiveness, then after a while He will **"give us over to a reprobate mind" (Romans 1:28) KJV.**

CHAPTER 7

⚜ ENCOURAGEMENT ⚜

Just as discouragement comes in many forms, so does encouragement. With the wide range of sources of encouragement, sports, music, books, Scripture, plays, mountain climbing, swimming, games....I wonder why so many people are discouraged.

Realistically, it is hard to stay encouraged in the face of "hard knocks" such as losing your job, foreclosure, divorce, death, and the economy, the way it is. In other words, there are many reasons why we can be discouraged. The mother eagle disturbs the nest after a while, to create unease and forces the eaglet out of the nest. I am sure the eaglet was not encouraged by that disturbance.

The Lord, Himself will at times, create unease in order to take you out of a comfort zone and stimulate growth. He will sometimes take away what used to make you content and comfortable.

Why did Jesus take the disciples out at sea, knowing that a storm was coming? Was it not to teach them about faith? If you desire to go to a higher place with God, be prepared because He will shift you out of a life of ease.

"As evening came, Jesus said to his disciples, "Let's cross to the other side of the lake." ³⁶ So they took Jesus in the boat and started out, leaving the crowds behind (although other boats followed). ³⁷ But soon a fierce storm came up. High waves were breaking into the boat, and it began to fill with water.

³⁸ Jesus was sleeping at the back of the boat with his head on a cushion. The disciples woke him up, shouting, "Teacher, don't you care that we're going to drown?"

³⁹ When Jesus woke up, he rebuked the wind and said to the waves, "Silence! Be still!" Suddenly the wind stopped, and there was a great calm. ⁴⁰ Then he asked them, "Why are you afraid? Do you still have no faith?"

⁴¹ The disciples were absolutely terrified. "Who is this man?" they asked each other. "Even the wind and waves obey him!" (Mark 4: 35-41) NLT.

As you mature in God, you will be able to deal with the issues of life with new perspective. When outside sources of encouragement dries up, like David you will come to a place where you realize that you have to encourage yourself in God. **"And David was greatly distressed; for the people spake of stoning him, because the soul of all the people was grieved, every man for his sons and for his daughters: but David encouraged himself in the LORD his God"** (1Samuel 30:6) KJV.

God described David as a man after His (God's) own heart, because he always desired to please God, albeit he "messed up" so many, many times. David had a sincere desire for worship. In the middle of desperate despair in the first two verses of Psalm 22, he went from a pitiful appeal to God for help, to a state of sheer worship as he acknowledged the awesomeness of God –"You are Holy."

His attitude was that in spite of what his circumstances looked like, he would acknowledge God's holiness, he would applaud Him, and he would worship Him.

"My God, my God, why have you abandoned me? Why are you so far away when I groan for help? Every day I call to you, my God, but you do not answer. Every night you hear my voice, but I find no relief. Yet you are holy, enthroned on the praises of Israel" (Psalm 22: 1-3) NLT.

BARUCH

Baruch was the Scribe who recorded on the Scroll for Jeremiah (Jeremiah 36:1-8). Baruch had long been serving this unpopular prophet, writing his book of struggles and judgments, and now he was upset (Jeremiah 45). Baruch was discouraged because he was fatigued and worn out with his depressive chores. God told Baruch to take his eyes off of himself and whatever rewards he thought he deserved. If Baruch did this God would protect him when disaster struck Israel.

It is easy to lose the joy of serving our God when we take our eyes off Him. The more we look away from God's purposes towards our own sacrifices, the more frustrated we will become. As you serve God beware of focusing on what you are giving up. When this happens, ask God's forgiveness; then look to Him rather than yourself. In spite of your failings, God gives forgiveness. He reassured Baruch.

"Are you seeking great things for yourself? Don't do it! I will bring great disaster upon all these people; but I will give you your life as a reward wherever you go. I, the LORD, have spoken!" (Jeremiah 45:5) NLT.

The New International Version says of verse 5. **"Wherever you go I will let you escape with your life."** What does escaping with your life mean? It does not mean that you will be spared the heat of the battle, and confrontation with the Enemy. It means you will be snatched out of the jaws of the Enemy, as David snatched the Lamb from the Lion.

It means a life preserved in the midst of continual pressure. It means comfort, reassurance, and hope from God in the midst of the dark times; times such as Paul and his friends experienced as they "were under great pressure that they despaired even of life" (2 Corinthians 1:8); pressures such as Paul experienced when the "thorn in the flesh" forced him to God asking that it be removed, but instead learning that God's "grace is sufficient" (2Corinthians 12:9).

We often pray to be delivered from afflictions, rather than asking God to make us what we ought to be. My prayer and focus lately is not for an easy life, but to be a stronger person in God. Great men of faith and endurance honored God and represented him well, not because they of themselves were so strong; but they were able to *endure* in the presence of their enemies because they *dwelt* in the presence of their God.

You may be a person of great influence, or you may be a person like Baruch who worked for a disliked employer like Jeremiah. If you remain faithful to the one who is set over you, and to the God who sees all things, the same message given to Baruch is applicable to you. As you go through the twists and turns of life, may you escape with your life wherever you go.

I have escaped with my life and view this as a lifelong message for me. **"A thick and dreadful darkness came over him"** (Genesis 15:12) NLT. As I read this passage, I remember New Year's Eve 2010 into 2011. This verse is a good description of my experience on that night. This verse in context was depicting Abraham's experience after he had spent the whole day making sacrifice to God on the altar, guarding the sacrifice from vultures, and was now exhausted.

Worn out from physical and mental exhaustion from the arduous labor of the day's work, Abraham fell into a deep sleep. His soul became tormented and oppressed, an oppression that seemed to smother him and brought a sense of torture to his heart (Genesis 15:12). I cannot say that I had sacrificed like Abraham did that day, nor can I say that my life over the years have qualified me to be in company with Abraham. What I can say is that the **"thick dreadful darkness"** perfectly describes the experience I had on that New Years Eve.

I was going through Chemotherapy at that time and because my immune system was extremely compromised by the Chemotherapy, I was forced to be house-bound for a long time or to wear a mask when I went out. It seemed like I entered into a "pity party" or something, because suddenly a frightening feeling, or sensation, or mindset overtook me that I could not get rid of. I felt like I was going down into a dark abyss at a rapid rate of speed and was powerless to stop it.

I mustered up all the Spiritual acumen I could but to no avail; I was weak. At twelve thirty that night, I got a prayer partner on the phone that travailed with me for many hours, until finally my release and breakthrough came at four o'clock in the morning. Thank God for faithful people who will come alongside a person in need.

Have you ever experienced such anguish? I know people have, after all, I am not singled out. Maybe you have gone through worse. Have you experienced a pain in your heart that caused you to wonder if the Lord has forsaken you? A pain that is difficult to reconcile with God's perfect love? This dilemma seems contradictory to "the peace of God that passes all human understanding" that God promises to give.

The sorrow of unkindness when you have extended your heart; the sorrow of betrayal when you have given complete trust; the sorrow of unfaithfulness when you have been loyal and would not dream of betraying trust, are some of the scenarios that could lead you into **"thick, heavy darkness."** When you get caught up in the jaws of such experiences, you wonder what suddenly broadsided you; you may even wonder if there is a God above who sees what is happening yet continues to allow it.

Be assured that God's divine justice is orchestrating His plan for the heart that is willing to continue trusting Him. May we realize that we always have hope in God. We have the "hope that anchors the soul, firm and secure while the billows roll." With the comfort that we have received when we have gone through, let us comfort and encourage others.

The worse place to be when the dark experiences strike is to think that the circumstances have separated you from God or to think that He is nowhere to be found. An even worse place is to think that God has forgotten you. To be at this vulnerable place is like being at a precipice.

This is imminent danger. This is where the Enemy whispers doubt in your mind and reinforce past failings making you feel "unqualified" for God's provisions. He is famous for asking this question, "If the Lord is with us, why is this happening to us?" (Judges: 6:13). Beloved, keep in mind and heart this truth; *your most amazing victory is born out of your deepest pain or disappointment.*

The Lord's message to Baruch was not to live in expectation that some great thing will come to him for the work that he had done. We too are to work for God and to give of ourselves without expecting rewards from mortal man. Sometimes we are tested to the point where the circumstances are unreasonable, and even then our expectation comes from God. **"My soul, wait thou only upon God; for my expectation is from him" (Psalm 62:5)** KJV.

"Fret not thyself because of evildoers, neither be thou envious against the workers of iniquity" (Psalm 37:1) KJV.

L.B.Cowman has a great analogy for what happens when we fret. *"Do not fret." Never get unduly upset! Stay cool! Even for a good reason, worrying will not help you. It only heats up the bearings but does not generate any steam. It does not help the Locomotive for its axels to become hot; their heat is only a hindrance. The axels become heated because of unnecessary friction. Dry surfaces are grinding against each other instead of working in smooth cooperation, aided by a thin cushion of oil.*

Isn't it interesting how similar the words "fret" and "friction" is? Friction caused by fretting is an indication of the absence of the anointing oil of the Grace of God. When we worry, a little bit of sand gets into the bearings. It may be some slight disappointment, ungratefulness, or discourtesy we have experienced – suddenly our life is not running smoothly. Friction leads to heat, and heat can lead to very dangerous conditions.

ANCHORED TO THE ROCK

One particular morning when I knelt at my bedside to pray, I had no words to verbalize so I just knelt there. Because I know that prayer does not necessarily mean talking, I knew that I had to wait on the Lord. This was not a new experience to me; in fact many times my mind wanders into many different things before I eventually get really focused on God. So this particular morning was not unusual.

As I knelt there, the refrain of a song came to me and I started to sing in my heart. *"Wrap me in your arms, wrap me in your arms, wrap me in your arms; Take me to that place Lord, to that secret place Lord, Where I can be with you and you can be with me."* And I continued singing.

I sang it over and over and as I sang, suddenly I saw myself clutching to the side of a cliff. I was holding on for dear life. This was a very high, mountainous cliff, and I was not standing on top, but holding on the jagged stones on the side. There was nowhere to anchor my feet or to get a good grip with my hands, so I held onto the rock with my fingers. Of course my fingers started slipping after a short time.

Because I tend to be acrophobic I could not look down and the wide expanse of the horizon told me that I was very high in the air. I could just look up; so I looked up and asked the Lord to save me. I then continued to sing the refrain, *"wrap me in your arms, wrap me in your arms, and wrap me in your arms."*

All day the song stayed with me. It brought me great comfort; the comfort I needed as I signed divorce papers later that day. It seems contradictory to be looking to the Lord and receiving from Him, comfort in the middle of an endeavor such as a divorce. Some may even venture to say that my experience on the cliff was an indication not to sign those papers, however I am convinced of the clearance that God had given to me that day regarding the relationship.

Over time the Lord has graciously given me insight to deal with some hard, painful, and difficult situations; insights that have helped to release me from what would otherwise ensnare me. What has helped me in this particular dilemma of facing an unpopular and unwelcome divorce is still unfolding.

The picture I got this morning of holding onto the Rock, reassured me that I am still anchored in God. I received it as confirmation that I am still well in spite of the tough decision I had to make regarding my marriage. The Lord prepared a friend to help me in understanding this.

CHAPTER 8

⋖I HAVE BEGUN TO DELIVER...⋗ NOW BEGIN TO POSSESS THAT YOU MAY INHERIT (DEUTERONOMY 2:31)

There is a natural law at work in Sin, Sickness, and the mundane order of things that when succumbed to leads to a state of passivity where the Tempter, Satan, dominates. But there is another order; a Spiritual order in Christ Jesus, which when attained actually counteracts the natural order that tend to naturally weigh us down.

The ugliness that is a part of my routine life I am able to counterbalance when I get into the Spiritual realm; reading the Word, listening to great sermons, listening to inspiring songs and hymns, fellowshipping with the believers, engaging in prayer, and doing the work of the Ministry.

This passage has helped me to take things in the perspective I have just described. It has become one of my favorite Scriptures as it got a hold of me at a time when I really needed to transition from looking at my circumstances that were draining me, and looking to God.

My God, my God, why hast thou forsaken me? Why art thou so far from helping me, and from the words of my roaring? O my God, I cry in the day time, but thou hearest not; and in the night season, and am not silent. But thou art holy, O thou that inhabitest the praises of Israel. (Psalm 22: 1-3) KJV.

In this Messianic psalm, David gave an amazingly accurate description of the suffering the Messiah would endure hundreds of years later. David was obviously enduring some great trial, but through his suffering, he, like the Messiah to come, gained victory. Jesus, the Messiah, quoted this verse while hanging on the cross carrying our burden of Sin (Matthew 27:46).

It was not a cry of doubt, but an urgent appeal to God. In spite of the reality of the present circumstances, we also can take our eyes off the situations long enough to look up and see God in His Holiness. When we get that sight of His holiness we, like Isaiah, will see our true selves and cry "Woe is me."

"Then said I, Woe is me! For I am undone; because I am a man of unclean lips, and I dwell in the midst of a people of unclean lips: for mine eyes have seen the King, the LORD of hosts" (Isaiah 6:5) KJV.

Counterbalancing the natural order and soaring in the Spirit takes intentionality. It will not just happen by chance. You have to swim against the natural currents of life. You have to take a stand that regardless of what the circumstances look like, God's way is best and you will follow it.

Last Wednesday, when I got finished with the work I volunteered to do at the Church, I walked out into the hallway and ran into my publisher, Sean Cort, and his mentor. He introduced me very graciously, explaining that I had just finished writing my autobiography "Nuggets....Along the Way" (www.trueperspectivepublishinghouse.com).

I explained how writing has been a very liberating experience for me and that the process has clarified my areas of ministry to hurting women and girls. He pronounced a blessing on me and said that because I have obeyed God in being courageous and transparent, that I will experience great blessings. He said that my family will be delivered, blessings will flow in my life, and that debts will be paid – even starting the same weekend. I became very emotional about this because I was at a most vulnerable place; a place I've never been before. I believe that I have been set up for great miracles.

THE CONFIRMATION

The day after I got this pronouncement over my life I got the confirmation which I hold dear to my heart. In my devotion, I read **"I have begun to deliver....now begin to conquer and possess" (Deuteronomy 2:31)**. I held on to every word of this Scripture and my devotional for January 26th. It is worth transcribing for you with the hope that it will bring you even half the encouragement that it brought me. It goes as follows:

*The Bible has a great deal to say about waiting for God, and the teaching cannot be too strongly emphasized. We so easily become impatient with God's delays. Yet much of our trouble in life is the result of our restless, and sometimes reckless, haste. We cannot **wait** for the fruit to ripen, but insist on picking it while it is still green. We cannot **wait** for answer to our prayers, although it may take many years for the things we pray for to be prepared for us. We are encouraged to walk with God, but often God walks very slowly. Yet there is also another side to this teaching:* **God often waits for us.**

*Quite often we fail to receive the blessing He has ready for us because we are not walking forward with Him. While it is true we miss many blessings by not **waiting** for God, we also miss numerous blessings by **over-waiting**. There are many times when it takes great strength simply to sit still, but there are also times when we are to move forward with a confident step.*

*Many of God's promises are conditional, requiring some initial action on our part. Once we begin to obey, He will begin to bless us. Great things were promised to Abraham, but not one of them could have been obtained had he waited in Chaldea. He had to leave his home, friends, and country, travel many unfamiliar paths, and press on in unwavering obedience in order to receive the promises. The ten lepers Jesus healed were told to show themselves to the priests, and **"as they went, they were cleansed" (Luke 17:14).** If they had waited to see the cleansing come to their bodies before leaving, they would never have seen it. God was **waiting to heal** them, and the moment their faith began to work, the blessing came.*

*When the Israelites were entrapped by Pharaoh's pursuing army at the Red Sea, they were commanded to **"go forward" (Exodus 14:15).** No longer was it their duty to wait, but to rise up from bended knees and **"go forward"** with heroic faith. Years later the Israelites were commanded to show their faith again by beginning their march over the Jordan while the river was at its highest point. They held the key to unlock the gate into the Land of Promise in their own hands, and the gate would not begin to turn on its hinges until they had approached and unlocked it. The Key was faith.*

We are destined to fight certain battles, and we think we can never be victorious and conquer our enemies. Yet, as we enter the conflict, **One** *comes to fight by our side. Through Him we are* **"more than conquerors"** *(Romans 8:37). If we had waited in fear and trembling for our Helper to come before we would enter the battle, we would have waited in vain. This would have been the* **over-waiting** *of unbelief. God is waiting to pour out His richest blessings on you."* **Go forward"** *with bold confidence and take what is yours. "I have begun to deliver…Now begin to conquer and possess." J.R. Miller.* **(Streams in the Desert)** *L.B. Cowman.*

A Surrendered Life

I have to surrender my life to God daily. I am acutely aware of my propensity to go astray and live according to my own understanding. I remember a Sermon preached many years ago, addressing the wanderings of Israel in the wilderness. At a point in the message the preacher challenged the audience on our own tendencies to wander. He told us not to be so quick in judging Israel because, in his own words **"we were they."** I have smiled at this over and over again. Paul in his writing to the Corinthians warned them of this.

"Nor should we put Christ to the test, as some of them did and then died from snakebites. And don't grumble as some of them did, and then were destroyed by the angel of death. These things happened to them as examples for us. They were written down to warn us who live at the end of the age. If you think you are standing strong, be careful not to fall" (1 Corinthians 10:9-12) NLT

This is what happened to Israel in the wilderness, and is a warning to us to take heed. The preacher was pointing out that we have the same tendency as Israel had. Israel did not have to spend 40 years on the way to the Promised Land. God sentenced them to wilderness wanderings because they rejected His love, rebelled against His authority, ignored His commands for right living, and willfully broke their end of the agreement made in Exodus 19:8 and Exodus 24: 3-8. In short, they disobeyed God.

I keep surrendering to God daily because if I walk in disobedience, like Israel did, I will not receive the promise. I purpose to "**possess that I will inherit**" the promise pronounced over my life. God has done His part; it is now up to me.

As I read the Scriptures around the verse, Deuteronomy 2:31, I realized that thirty eight years had already passed since the children of Israel started in the wilderness. The people of Israel would sin and repent, murmur and repent, and sin again. God, in His mercy showed compassion on them and offered them forgiveness.

God showed Israel favor in defending them against their enemies. "**Beginning today I will make people throughout the earth terrified because of you. When they hear reports about you, they will tremble with dread and fear**" (Deuteronomy 2:25) NLT.

We are no match for the enemy, but God is; and as He did for Israel, He wants to do for each and every one of us, if we will allow Him. God told Moses that He would make the enemy nations afraid of Israel. By worldly standards, Israel's army was not intimidating, but Israel had God on its side.

Moses no longer had to worry about his enemies because his enemies were worried about him. God often goes before us in our daily battles, preparing the way and overcoming barriers. The ones He allows us to deal with are the ones that He has determined are necessary for our growth and development. We need to follow Him wholeheartedly and be alert to His leading.

When we have been prepared by the means that God has allowed in our lives, and we have heard His command to advance, we can be assured that all is well. Moses heard the Word that God had begun to deliver and that he and Israel should **possess** so that they could **inherit**. I have heard that same Word for my life.

Dictionary.com. describes these words as follows.

Possess: Have as belonging to one; own. Have possession of as distinct from ownership.

Inherit: To take or receive property or the like by virtue of being heir to it. To receive qualities, powers, duties, etc., as by inheritance. To have succession as heir.

Israel had big challenges and faced large armies that they had no chance against. They won because God fought for them. God can help His people regardless of what challenges they face. No matter how insurmountable the obstacles may seem, remember that God is sovereign and He will keep His promises. Like Israel, after we have endured, He will establish us. Let us make good use of our inheritance. Let us go in and possess.

> *Life is not defined by what we go through, but by how we come out on the other side.* ~ Dr. Clinton Simms.

"In his kindness God called you to share in his eternal glory by means of Christ Jesus. So after you have suffered a little while, he will restore, support, and strengthen you, and he will place you on a firm foundation" (1 Peter 5:10) NLT.

"Though I have afflicted thee, I will afflict thee no more" (Nahum 1:12) KJV.

"The Lord of the harvest" (Luke 10:2) is not always threshing us. His trials are only for a season, and the showers soon pass. "Weeping may endure for a night, but rejoicing comes in the morning" (Psalm 30:5). "Our light, momentary troubles are achieving for us an eternal glory that far outweighs them all" (2Corinthians 4:17). Trials do serve their purpose.

Even the fact that we face a trial proves there is something very precious to our Lord in us, or else He would not spend so much time and energy on us. Christ would not test us if He did not see the precious metal of faith mingled with the rocky core of our nature, and it is to refine us into purity and beauty, that He forces us through the fiery ordeal. L.B. Cowman

Cowman wrote that the reason we are generally so easily sidetracked by difficulties is that we expect to see barriers removed before we even try to pass through them. The barriers of our lives are the stone that we have to step on to get to a higher place in God. If they are removed then we will not step higher.

We are required to move straight ahead in faith; that is what the barriers are there for ~ to engender faith. True love motivates us to give of ourselves. Love causes us to commit. Commitment causes us to endure. When we endure, we persevere to the end:

> *O Love that wilt not let me go,*
> *I rest my weary soul in thee;*
> *I give thee back the life I owe,*
> *That in thine ocean depths its flow*
> *May richer, fuller be. George Mattheson*

Christopher Columbus taught a great lesson to the world on perseverance in the middle of tremendous difficulties. He taught us how to possess and to inherit.

Columbus
by Joaquin Miller

Behind him lay the gray Azores,
Behind the Gates of Hercules;
Before him not the ghost of shores;
Before him only shoreless seas.
The good mate said: "Now must we pray,
For lo! the very stars are gone.
Brave Admiral, speak, what shall I say?"
"Why, say : 'Sail on! sail on! and on!'"

"My men grow mutinous day by day;
My men grow ghastly, wan and weak."
The stout mate thought of home; a spray
Of salt wave washed his swarthy cheek.
What shall I say , brave Admiral, say,
If we sight naught but seas at dawn?"
"Why, you shall say at break of day,
'Sail on! sail on! sail on! and on!'"

They sailed and sailed, as winds might blow,
Until at last the blanched mate said:
"Why, now not even God would know
Should I and all my men fall dead.
These very winds forget their way,
For God from these dread seas is gone.
Now speak, brave Admiral, speak and say" --
He said: "Sail on! sail on! and on!"

They sailed. They sailed. Then spake the mate:
"This mad sea shows his teeth tonight.
He curls his lip, he lies in wait,
With lifted teeth, as if to bite!
Brave Admiral, say but one good word:
What shall we do when hope is gone?"
The words leapt like a leaping sword:
"Sail on! sail on! sail on! and on!"

Then, pale and worn, he paced his deck,
And peered through darkness. Ah, that night
Of all dark nights! And then a speck --
A light! A light! At last a light!
It grew, a starlit flag unfurled!
It grew to be Time's burst of dawn.
He gained a world; he gave that world
Its grandest lesson: "On! sail on!"

CHAPTER 9

✥ IF I HAVE FOUND FAVOR IN ✥ THY SIGHT, THEN SHOW ME THY WAYS (EXODUS 33:13)

It is easy to get into a life of complacency when everything is going well with us. However beyond a certain point, a life of ease can leave us unchallenged, unmotivated, apathetic, dull, indifferent, ordinary, unambitious, uncreative, unimaginative, and downright lazy.

Yet, our desire is to live in comfort and ease and that is what we all strive for in life. That is the reason why from a young age, our families instill in us the need to achieve a good education, which leads to a good job, which leads to a good paycheck, which leads to the ability to make a good life for our families; a life of comfort and ease. This is the Natural Life.

The opposite is also true. When faced with challenges, disputes, questions, confrontations, demands, interrogations, objections, provocations, tests, threats, trials, and ultimatums we are suddenly thrown into an uncomfortable situation where we have to "sink or swim." Suddenly we are forced to pull on all the resources we can muster up; we are forced to get two jobs, do a class on parenting, join Alcoholic Anonymous, find the Altar to pray, beg help from family....

At the end of this testing, especially if it is severe, we find that we have changed and will never be the same again. We have grown to a higher level in endurance, knowledge, and hopefully wisdom. I heard a statement a while ago that says; *an item that is stretched beyond a certain point will never return to its original position.* In order to grow we have to be stretched beyond that certain point, and from time to time God in His wisdom and love decides that it's time to be stretched. This usually encourages a search for Spiritual Truths.

Oh, how the old harpist loves his harp! He cuddles and caresses it, as if it was a child resting on his lap. His life is consumed with it. But watch how he tunes it. He grasps it firmly, striking a chord with a sharp, quick blow. While it quivers as if in pain, he leans forward, intently listening to catch the first note rising from it. Just as he feared, the note is distorted and shrill. He strains the string, turning the torturing thumbscrew, and though it seems ready to snap with the tension, he strikes it again. Then he leans forward again, carefully listening, until at last a smile appears on his face as the first melodic sounds arise. L.B.Cowman.

A LOOK AT ELIJAH

Maybe this is how God is dealing with you. If it is, you are in good company. Many have gone on ahead of you and many will follow when you are gone. Elijah was stretched to a point where he despaired for life. He was running away from Jezebel and found refuge in a cave. Ironically, this came just after God had used him to do one of the greatest miracles of his career (1Kings 18 &19).

But God, the greatest harpist, was stringing his harp even as He showed him mercy. He will not pull the string beyond that certain point of endurance. After you have endured, God will refresh, restore, and establish you just like He did for Elijah (1Kings 19).

"Then the LORD told him, "Go back the same way you came, and travel to the wilderness of Damascus. When you arrive there, anoint Hazael to be king of Aram. [16] Then anoint Jehu grandson of Nimshi to be king of Israel, and anoint Elisha son of Shaphat from the town of Abel-meholah to replace you as my prophet. [17] Anyone who escapes from Hazael will be killed by Jehu, and those who escape Jehu will be killed by Elisha! [18] Yet I will preserve 7,000 others in Israel who have never bowed down to Baal or kissed him!" (1Kings 19:15-18) NLT.

Isn't it just like God, whose "ways are higher than our ways" to send Elijah back the same way he came? He was running from danger, and here it is God is sending him back. But ah! Where God sends you, He equips you. There are many accounts of Elijah's work as he faithfully served God.

By and by he learned more and more about God's ways. He was not satisfied with getting favors from God. For his faithfulness, Elijah did not pass through a physical death, but was translated and taken up into heaven.

"As they were walking along and talking, suddenly a chariot of fire appeared, drawn by horses of fire. It drove between the two men, separating them, and Elijah was carried by a whirlwind into heaven" (2Kings 2: 11) NLT.

A LOOK AT SOLOMON

Solomon, the wisest man who ever lived described our ambitious efforts in life like this; **"Everything is meaningless ...completely meaningless!"** (Ecclesiastes 1:2) NLT. He continued to ponder the controversies of life as "history repeating itself" (Vs 9), and that "nothing is new under the sun" (vs. 10). He further gave us much to think about in the rest of the chapter and in fact in the whole book of Ecclesiastes.

"I said to myself, "Look, I am wiser than any of the kings who ruled in Jerusalem before me. I have greater wisdom and knowledge than any of them." So I set out to learn everything from wisdom to madness and folly. But I learned firsthand that pursuing all this is like chasing the wind. The greater my wisdom, the greater my grief; to increase knowledge only increases sorrow" (Ecclesiastes 116-18) NLT

The ways of God is far beyond the minds of mortal man, including the wisest man that ever lived.

"My thoughts are nothing like your thoughts," says the LORD. "And my ways are far beyond anything you could imagine. For just as the heavens are higher than the earth, so my ways are higher than your ways and my thoughts higher than your thoughts" (Isaiah 55: 8-9) NLT

The wisest man has a word for the "wise" and for all whose sole purpose is to pursue the natural ambitions of life. After he had wondered and pondered and wondered again, he had this conclusion.

"But, my child let me give you some further advice: Be careful, for writing books is endless, and much study wears you out. That's the whole story. Here now is my final conclusion: Fear God and obey his commands, for this is everyone's duty. God will judge us for everything we do, including every secret thing, whether good or bad" (Ecclesiastes 12: 12-14) NLT.

When anointed as a young king over Israel, Solomon had previously asked God for favor to lead the people. Understandable, he was overwhelmed and worried, wondering if he was able to do the job. Solomon asked; **"Give me the wisdom and knowledge to lead them properly, for who could possibly govern this great people of yours?"**

God answered him affirmatively. **"Because your greatest desire is to help your people, and you did not ask for wealth, riches, fame, or even the death of your enemies or a long life, but rather you asked for wisdom and knowledge to properly govern my people—I will certainly give you the wisdom and knowledge you requested. But I will also give you wealth, riches, and fame such as no other king has had before you or will ever have in the future!"** (2Chronicles1: 10-12) NLT.

Solomon enjoyed a peaceful and prosperous reign for forty years that made him world famous. His greatest achievement was to build the temple of God that his father was not allowed to build because he was regarded as a man of war. The temple was the religious center of the nation and signified the unity of the tribes, the presence of God among the people, and the nation's high calling to be an example to other nations.

We can achieve great thing in life, but we must never neglect any effort that will help nurture God's people or bring others into God's kingdom. It is easy for us to get the wrong perspective as to what is really important in life. Solomon stayed focused to the task.

Solomon was faithful to fulfill God's requirement for building the temple, but was weak in his relationships; he married many pagan women which eventually led to his downfall.

A LOOK AT MOSES

In the same way Solomon sought God for direction to rule the people of Israel; Moses had sought God many years earlier. When we read the story of these lives, we can readily see that they were imperfect men such as we are, yet God gave Solomon, not just the wisdom he asked for, but great riches and wealth beyond any other king of his day and even to this day.

He found favor with God because of his humility, but later fell into sin and had to be disciplined severely by God. Moses was prepared for service when he was found out for killing an Egyptian (Exodus 2: 14). He had to run away but found refuge in Midian, where he settled down, got married and started a family. Years later God sent him back to Egypt to deliver Israel from the bondage of slavery.

Some people can't stay out of trouble. When conflicts break out, they always manage to be nearby. Reaction is their favorite action. This was Moses. He seemed drawn to what needed to be righted. Throughout his life, he was at his finest and his worst while responding to the conflicts around him.

He was definitely not called to live of ease and comfort. Even the burning Bush experience (Exodus 3) was an illustration of his character. Having spotted the fire and seen that the bush did not burn, he had to investigate. Whether jumping into a fight to defend a Hebrew slave or trying to referee a struggle between two kinsmen, when Moses saw conflict, he reacted.

Over the years, however, an amazing thing happened to Moses character. He didn't stop reacting, but rather learned to respond correctly. The challenge of leading a nation of millions of sometimes rebellious people through the wilderness was more than enough challenge to straighten out Moses leading abilities.

One moment he was being an intercessor, pleading the people's case to God; at another moment he had to respond to the peoples bickering and complaining; yet another moment he had to respond to their unjustified accusations against him; then he had to deal with his partner, Aaron's lack of good judgment.

Moses was an outstanding leader. In Moses we see an outstanding personality shaped by God. We must not misunderstand what God did. He did not change who or what Moses was; He did not give Moses new abilities and strengths. Instead He took Moses characteristics and molded them until they were suited to His purposes. Likewise God will use the characteristics He has given to you and mold them for His purposes, if you are willing. He is taking take what He created in the first place, and using it for His intended purpose.

Moses was mightily used by God and was called a man of God. He found favor with God and wanted to understand God more. One day he said to God **"If it is true that you look favorably on me, let me know your ways so I may understand you more fully" (Exodus 33:13) NLT.**

This is obviously a man who is seeking, not just the benefits from God, but desiring his company; desiring a relationship. That's really what God wants of us. We too have to come to a place in our lives where we look beyond a comfortable life of God's favor, and look for God's purpose for our lives.

God and Moses would talk face to face in the tabernacle of the congregation, as friends (Exodus 33). Why did Moses find such favor with God? It certainly was not because he was perfect, gifted or powerful. Rather, it was because, God chose Moses, and Moses in turn relied wholeheartedly on God's wisdom and direction. This it is not out of reach for us today. Jesus called His disciples-and by extension, all of His followers- His friends (John 15:15). Will you trust Him as Moses did and be called His friend?

The desire in Moses heart was not to see miracles, just to see the spectacular, but he sincerely had a desire to understand the ways of God, **"let me know your ways so I may understand you more fully"**. It takes people who are set apart, or who have attained a special place in God, to know the ways of God.

An average person could not understand, even if it was given to them. The average person is satisfied with the acts of God. They like to see the spectacular, but are not prepared to go through the discipline necessary to go to a higher place where they can learn His ways. **"He revealed his character to Moses and his deeds to the people of Israel" (Psalm 103:7) NLT.**

Moses was rewarded for seeking diligently after God's ways; he was given a shielded view of the glory of God from the cleft in the rock. No one could see the full glory of God and live. Moses' prayer was to see the manifest glory of God. He wanted assurance of God's presence with him, Aaron and Joshua, and also he wanted to know that presence experientially. Because we are finite and morally imperfect, we cannot see God as He is, and continue to live. Moses saw God's backside, which meant that he could see only where God had passed by. He could not see the full view of God.

The LORD replied, "I will make all my goodness pass before you, and I will call out my name, Yahweh, before you ..... I will hide you in the crevice of the rock and cover you with my hand until I have passed by. Then I will remove my hand and let you see me from behind. But my face will not be seen" (Exodus 33: 17-23) NLT.

Moses, obviously found great favor with God. However later on in his journey with leading Israel through the wilderness, he came into a difficult time where he got angry and walked out of obedience with God. He was severely punished. Although the people, many times, rebelled against Moses leadership, God did not excuse him when he got angry out of frustration against the people and sinned.

"And Moses and Aaron gathered the congregation together before the rock, and he said unto them, Hear now, ye rebels; must we fetch you water out of this rock? And Moses lifted up his hand, and with his rod he smote the rock twice: and the water came out abundantly, and the congregation drank, and their beasts also" (Numbers 20: 9-11) KJV.

Because of his disobedience, Moses was forbidden to enter the promise land. He could only look at it from afar.

A LOOK AT JESUS' RELATIONSHIP WITH US – *HIS DISCIPLES*

We cannot comprehend God, as He is, apart from Jesus Christ (John 14: 9). Jesus promised to show Himself to those who love Him (John 14:21).

One day Jesus was telling His disciples that He was going away to the Father, and He was going to prepare a place for them. He told them that He was the only way to the Father. Thomas and Phillip had many questions about this and Phillip said **"Lord, show us the Father, and we will be satisfied."**

To this Jesus replied:

"Jesus replied, "Have I been with you all this time, Philip, and yet you still don't know who I am? Anyone who has seen me has seen the Father! So why are you asking me to show him to you?" (John 14:9) NLT.

We do not have to worry and fret that we will not see the Father. If we choose to acknowledge that we are sinners, repent of our Sin and accept Jesus Christ as our Lord and Savior, then we are showing God that we love His son Jesus; then we have Salvation. At this point we are entitled to the same promises that Jesus gave to His disciples.

"Those who accept my commandments and obey them are the ones who love me. And because they love me, my Father will love them and I will love them and reveal myself to each of them" (John 14:21) NLT.

Sometimes people wish they knew the future, so they could prepare for it. God has chosen not to give us this knowledge. He alone knows what will happen, but He tells us all we need to know to prepare for the future. When we live by His standards' He will not leave us; He will come to us, He will be in us, and He will show Himself to us. God knows what will happen, and He will be with us through it all, we need not fear.

We don't have to know the future to have faith in God; we have to have faith in God to be secure about the future. Jesus said that His followers show their love for Him by obeying Him. Love is more than lovely words; it is commitment and conduct. If you love Christ, then prove it by obeying what He says in His Word.

The same expectations that God had of these men described above, are the same that He requires of us. God knows where we are, and He knows what we can endure. He has determined that our faith must be stretched in order to grow; **"These trials will show that your faith is genuine. It is being tested as fire tests and purifies gold—though your faith is far more precious than mere gold" (1Peter 1:7) NLT.**

Just like God allowed the Enemy to test Job, He determines that there are some hardships that are necessary for you and me. Daniel had his own set of drama in the lion's den (Daniel 6); Shadrach, Meshach, and Abednego had their concerns while they were bound and thrown into the fire, while remaining faithful to God. They said in faith;

"Shadrach, Meshach, and Abednego replied, "O Nebuchadnezzar, we do not need to defend ourselves before you. [17] If we are thrown into the blazing furnace, the God whom we serve is able to save us. He will rescue us from your power, Your Majesty. [18] But even if he doesn't, we want to make it clear to you, Your Majesty, that we will never serve

your gods or worship the gold statue you have set up" (Daniel 3: 16-18) NLT.

If God always rescued those who were true to Him, Christians would not need faith. Our religion would be a great Insurance Policy, and there would be lines of selfish people ready to sign up. We must be faithful to serve God whether He intervene on our behalf or not. Our eternal rewards are worth any suffering we may have to endure first.

Chapter 10

❧ You were born for this. ❧ "This is my doing" (1 Kings 12:24)

The disappointments of life are simply the hidden appointments of love. C.A. Fox.

My child, I have a message for you today. Let me whisper it in you ear so any storm clouds that may arise will shine with glory, and the rough places you may have to walk will be made smooth. It is only four words, but let them sink into your inner being, and use them as a pillow to rest your weary head. **"This is my doing."**

Have you ever realized that whatever concerns you concerns me too? "For whoever touches you touches the apple of [my] eye" (Zechariah 2:8). "You are precious and honored in my sight" (Isaiah 43:4). Therefore it is my special delight to teach you.

I want you to learn when temptations attack you, and the Enemy comes in "like a pent-up flood" (Isaiah 59:19), that **"this is** *my doing"* and that your weakness needs My Strength, and your safety lies in letting Me fight for you.

Are you in difficult circumstances, surrounded by people who do not understand you, never ask your opinion, and always push you aside? **"This is my doing."** I am the God of circumstances. You did not come to this place by accident – you are exactly where I meant for you to be.

Have you not ask me to make you humble? Then see that I have placed you in the perfect school where this lesson is taught. Your circumstances and the people around you are only being used to accomplish My will.

Are you having problems with money, finding it hard to make ends meet? **"This is my doing,"** for I am the one who keeps your finances, and I want you to learn to depend upon Me. My supply is limitless and I "will meet all your needs" (Philippians 4:19). I want you to prove My promises so no one may say, "You did not trust in the Lord your God" (Deuteronomy 1:32).

Are you experiencing a time of sorrow? **"This is my doing."** I am "a man of sorrow, and familiar with suffering" (Isaiah 53:3) I have allowed your earthly comforters to fail you, so that by turning to Me you may receive "eternal encouragement and good hope" (2 Thessalonians 2:16). Have you longed to do some great work for me but instead have been set aside on a bed of sickness and pain? **"This is my doing."**

You were so busy, I could not get your attention, and I wanted to teach you some of my deepest truths. "They also serve who only stand and wait." In Fact, some of My greatest workers *are those physically unable to serve, but who have learned to wield the powerful weapon of prayer.*

Today I place a cup of Holy Oil in your hands. Use it freely, My child. Anoint with it, every new circumstance, every word that hurts you, every interruptions that makes you impatient, and every weakness you have. The pain will leave as you learn to see Me in all things. Laura A. Barter Snow.

It is so easy to miss the moving of God. His works are many times delayed, hidden, painful, seemingly contradictory and controversial, and definitely unpopular. God's ways are definitely not what the natural man desires. It is not satisfying to the natural instinct, so everything about the natural person rebels against it. The Scriptures tell us that God's ways are not our ways.

"My thoughts are nothing like your thoughts," says the LORD. "And my ways are far beyond anything you could imagine. For just as the heavens are higher than the earth, so my ways are higher than your ways and my thoughts higher than your thoughts" (Isaiah 55: 8-9) NLT

"Those who are spiritual can evaluate all things, but they themselves cannot be evaluated by others. For who can know the Lord's thoughts? Who knows enough to teach him?"

But we understand these things, for we have the mind of Christ" (1 Corinthians 2:15-16) NLT

We are also reassured that we have the mind of Christ. We are actually in great company. However, we are foolish to think that we know how God will act at any given time. We cannot act like we know what God is planning or thinking, because His knowledge and wisdom is far beyond us. We must strive to fit into His plan and purpose rather than the other way around.

Non-Christians cannot understand Spiritual truths, and they cannot grasp the concept that God's Spirit lives in believers. Don't expect most people to approve of or to understand your decision to follow Christ. It all seems so silly to them. Just like a tone-deaf person cannot understand fine music, the person who rejects Christ cannot understand the truths from God's Spirit. With the lines of communication broken, he or she won't be able to hear what God is saying to him or her.

No one can know what God is thinking (Romans 11:34), but through the guidance of the Holy Spirit, believers have insight into some of God's plans, thought and actions. They "have the mind of Christ" because of the Holy Spirit. Through the Holy Spirit, we can begin to know God's thoughts, talk with Him, and expects His answers to our prayers. Are you spending enough time with Christ to have His very mind in you? An intimate relationship with Christ comes only from spending time consistently in His presence and in His word. And Yes! You were born for this.

To live for the Lord and to gain momentum on a journey with Him, you have to be born again; acknowledge yourself as a sinner, ask Jesus to forgive you of your sins and to come into your heart and live, and you will develop a Kingdom mindset. Developing a Kingdom mindset is accepting the Scriptures as the inspired Word of God and the road map for the journey, being diligent in following the road map and listening to the tour guide, the Holy Spirit, and walking in obedience to the Word.

Sometimes the circumstances in which we find ourselves scream at us that it is impossible to be all that God desires us to be; but we were actually born for this and God has made provisions for us along the way. The Scriptures give us check points along the way, refreshing for the journey, and reassurance that God has already placed eternity in our hearts. We just have to be willing and for sure He is able. **"Yet God has made everything beautiful for its own time. He has planted eternity in the human heart, but even so, people cannot see the whole scope of God's work from beginning to end"** (Ecclesiastes 3: 11) NLT.

He has invested much in us and He requires much from us. He expect for His children to step up and take hold of His promises and do what is required to succeed in Him.

The roadmap, the Scriptures, tell us to set our hearts, mind, and affections on Him. **"Since you have been raised to new life with Christ, set your sights on the realities of heaven, where Christ sits in the place of honor at God's right hand. Think about the things of heaven, not the things of earth"** (Colossians 31-2) NLT

You have a choice to live a purpose-filled life in God. To achieve this you have to subject yourself to a daily surrendering of your natural tendencies and depend on the Holy Spirit to mold you and make you after His will. Jesus said **"If any man will come after me, let him deny himself, and take up his cross daily, and follow me"** (Luke 9:23) KJV.

Your own mindset and abilities cannot achieve Spiritual things. The best of our abilities amounts to nothing; **"But we are all as an unclean thing, and all our righteousnesses are as filthy** rags; and we all do fade as a leaf; and our iniquities, like the wind, have taken us away" (Isaiah 64:6) KJV.

Because of the entry of Sin into the world, and eternal death (separation from God) because of Sin, we have no hope of eternal life (life with God) except through accepting Jesus Christ as Lord and Savior. None is exempt from this route. We have all sinned we all need forgiveness and redemption. **"For all have sinned, and come short of the glory of God" (Romans 3:23) KJV.**

We have not been left without hope as God provided a way to redeem, or buy, us back to himself; **"For the wages of sin is death; but the gift of God is eternal life through Jesus Christ our Lord" (Roman 6:23) KJV.**

This is what you and I were born for; to live a life with God. On our journey on this side of eternity, we have to deal with Sin and the effect of Sin in our lives. We cannot navigate our way through the labyrinth of troubles without the guidance and leading of the Holy Spirit. We are commanded to **"Trust in the LORD with all thine heart; and lean not unto thine own understanding. In all thy ways acknowledge him, and he shall direct thy paths" (Proverbs 3: 5-6) KJV.**

It's Not About You

Every day we see issues that we cannot reconcile. We hear questions that we cannot answer and have problems without solutions. This was not in our plans. Out of the blue unforeseen situations pop up into our lives and we are forced to handle it whether we like it or not. Everything within us cries out "this is not fair." Yes! Life is definitely not fair.

But what can anyone of us do about it? The hard questions that we hear from time to time are without reasonable answers. Questions like; why does God allow this or that? Why do bad things happen to good people?

This man was very angry after the death of his son. He had unanswered questions as to why God allowed it to happen. He could not be comforted. Days passed as he stewed in his sorrow, while well-meaning supporters tried to comfort him. A friend tried to direct him to the comfort that God gives, at which he let out all his pent-up anger; you see, his anger was with God because he expected God to intervene on his behalf and was most disappointed when it did not happen his way. He blurted out;

"Where was God when my son was dying?"

Led by the Holy Spirit, the man replied,

"God was in the same place He was when His own Son was being crucified."

This became a defining moment in the man's life and he was never the same; in fact, his whole perspective of life changed. He realized that picture-perfect, comfy, guaranteed life-style that he envisioned was really his superficial dream, and that there was more beyond his imagination that God wants to achieve in Him. He realized that the circumstances that he comes upon in his life are not always about him, but more so what God desires to accomplish in and through him.

GOD CAN USE ANYTHING

On our own merit we are not useable; in fact, if based on our education, looks, wits, achievements, status, money, heritage, or alliances, we believe that we are fit to be used of God, then we have completely missed the mark. This is pride at its zenith. **"God opposes the proud but favors the humble" (1Peter 5:5)** NLT. God chooses to use the simple things of life to do great and otherwise impossible tasks.

"Remember, dear brothers and sisters, that few of you were wise in the world's eyes or powerful or wealthy when God called you. Instead, God chose things the world considers foolish in order to shame those who think they are wise. And he chose things that are powerless to shame those who are powerful. God chose things despised by the world, things counted as nothing at all, and used them to bring to nothing what the world considers important" (1 Corinthians 1:26-28) NLT.

God will use whatever is available and do according to His choosing. He will even use our "mess" after we have surrendered ourselves to Him, repent, and ask His forgiveness. God will use our rebellious actions as a refining discipline. Even believers who choose to stray from His guidance, He allows to sin and then face the consequences of their actions. God allows this for several reasons;

- To show us our potential for sinning
- To encourage us to turn from Sin and constantly depend on Him
- To prepare us to face other, even stronger temptations in the future
- To help us to stay faithful and keep on trusting Him
- To encourage others in avoiding the pitfalls along the way

KING DAVID

God taught King David a hard lesson in 2 Samuel 24. God allowed David to take a census of the people, and then used this experience as a discipline for both David and Israel. Did God cause David to sin (vs. 1)?

Will God allow His people to Sin? God does not cause people to Sin; however because He has given us a free will, and thus choice, He will allow His people to Sin and learn from their wrongs. God does not cause people to Sin, but He does allow sinners to reveal the sinfulness of their hearts by their actions. This revelation is not for God's benefit, but for the sinner to see himself.

God presented the opportunity to David in order to deal with a disastrous national tendency, and He wanted this sinful desire to show itself. David at this time was getting prideful, as He and Israel were regarded as a formidable force by other nations. David wanted to glory in the size of his military strength, and was now substituting this for God.

This experience was not all about David, as you can see. The consequences were very disastrous (three days of plague on Israel vs. 15), but David and Israel came to a place of repentance and thus received forgiveness. It was not just for them then, but still speaks volumes to us now. This is where God desires all His people to be; at a place of repentance and surrender.

Many times the circumstances that we come upon are not about us. We are so self-centered that we can only see where the issue affects us, but we are not remotely aware that there could be other variables involved in the picture. The life of a child of God is not one of ease and comfort.

In fact, the promises of God that are available for us, for the most part, can be realized only when we are in the deep "flood waters." I have personally experienced the best of God when I have been at my wits end. Many Scriptures bear out the fact that we will go through tough times, so there is no doubt that tough times will come. But our confidence is that God will use the difficulties for our advantage.

But now, O Jacob, listen to the LORD who created you. O Israel, the one who formed you says, "Do not be afraid, for I have ransomed you. I have called you by name; you are mine. When you go through deep waters, I will be with you. When you go through rivers of difficulty, you will not drown. When you walk through the fire of oppression, you will not be burned up;
the flames will not consume you. For I am the LORD, your God, the Holy One of Israel, your Savior" (Isaiah 43: 1-3) NLT.

Will you let the Lord use your tough times to bring you to a higher place in Him? Will you let Him bring you into your destiny through a purpose-filled journey? The process is difficult but there is great rewards awaiting you.

"And since we are his children, we are his heirs. In fact, together with Christ we are heirs of God's glory. But if we are to share his glory, we must also share his suffering.
Yet what we suffer now is nothing compared to the glory he will reveal to us later. For all creation is waiting eagerly for that future day when God will reveal who his children really are" (Romans 8: 17-19) NLT.

PAUL

The patriarchs of old endured great hardships and we are here today to read about them. It was not all about them. Most times it was not about them at all. I have many favorites, but Paul is one of those that stands out. There are many accounts of his achievements in spite of his tumultuous life. Although Paul was denied the comforts and the natural means to make him contented, yet he was able to write this verse from a dark prison.

"Not that I was ever in need, for I have learned how to be content with whatever I have. [12] I know how to live on almost nothing or with everything. I have learned the secret of living in every situation, whether it is with a full stomach or empty, with plenty or little. For I can do everything through Christ, who gives me strength" (Philippians 4: 11-13) NLT.

Paul was able to see life from God's point of view. Paul knew how to be content whether he had plenty or whether he was in need. The secret is drawing on Christ's power for strength. If you always want more, ask God to remove that desire and teach you contentment in every situation.

Paul focused on what he was supposed to do rather than what he thought he should have. Often the desire to have more or better possessions is really a longing to fill an empty place in a person's life. How can you find true contentment? The answer lies in your perspective, your priorities, and your source of power. It was not all about Paul. It was all about what God wanted to accomplish through Paul.

What a legacy he has left for us?

- Paul was transformed by God from a persecutor of Christians to a preacher for Christ
- He preached for Christ throughout the Roman Empire on three missionary journeys
- He wrote letters to various churches, which became part of the New Testament
- He was never afraid to face an issue head-on and deal with it
- He was sensitive to God's leading, and despite his strong personality, always did as God directed

Prior to his conversion, Paul persecuted the Church of God and killed many Christians. He even approved and witnessed the stoning and killing of the apostle Stephen. In spite of this we learn the good news of forgiveness through Paul's life. God forgave him and used him in a mighty way to preach the same gospel he once killed people for preaching. God will use our past and our present so we can serve Him with our future.

It gives me great relief to know that my life is not just comprised of suffering. Sometimes it seems like God delights in causing His people harm, but I have been in this journey with the Lord long enough to know from experience that He does "turn sorrow into joy" (Esther 9:22&Jeremiah 31:13) and "gives beauty for ashes"(Isaiah 61:3). Our God is not a sadist. He loves us and wants the best for us. Unfortunately, the best for us most often cause us pain and suffering in this life, but everlasting joy for eternity. **"For I reckon that the sufferings of this present time are not worthy to be compared with the glory which shall be revealed in us" (Romans 8:18) KJV.**

We are reassured that our struggles will work for us praise, glory and honor at Christ's appearing. Isn't that the greatest hope we could ever have?

"So be truly glad. There is wonderful joy ahead, even though you have to endure many trials for a little while. These trials will show that your faith is genuine. It is being tested as fire tests and purifies gold—though your faith is far more precious than mere gold. So when your faith remains strong through many trials, it will bring you much praise and glory and honor on the day when Jesus Christ is revealed to the whole world" (1 Peter 1: 6 -7) NLT.

GOD WILL CAUSE YOU TO SOAR TO HIGH HEIGHTS.

"Then shalt thou delight thyself in the LORD; and I will cause thee to ride upon the high places of the earth, and feed thee with the heritage of Jacob thy father: for the mouth of the LORD hath spoken it" (Isaiah 58:14) KJV.

One of the first rules of aerodynamics is that flying into the wind quickly increases altitude. The wings of the airplane create more lift by flying against the wind. How was this lesson learned? It was learned by watching birds fly. If a bird is simply flying for pleasure, it flies with the wind. But if it senses danger, it turns into the wind to gain altitude, and flies up toward the sun.

The sufferings of life are God's winds. Sometimes they blow against us and are very strong. They are like hurricanes, taking our lives to higher levels, towards His heavens.

Do you remember a summer day when the heat and humidity were so oppressive, you could hardly breathe? But a dark cloud appeared on the horizon, growing larger and larger, until it suddenly brought a rich blessing to your world. The storm raged, lightening flashed, and thunder rumbled. The storm covered your sky, the atmosphere was cleansed, new life was in the air, and your world was changed.

Human life works exactly on the same principle. When the storms of life appear, the atmosphere is changed, purified, filled with new life, and part of heaven is brought down to earth. (Selected)

Facing obstacles should make us sing. The wind finds its voice not when rushing across an open sea but when it is hindered by the outstretched limb of a pine tree or broken by the strings of an Aeolian wind harp. Only then does the harp have songs of power and beauty.

Send your soul, which has been set free, sweeping across the obstacles of life. Send it through the relentless forests of pain and against even the smallest hindrances and worries of life, and it too will find a voice with which to sing. (Selected)

> **Be like a bird that, halting in its flight,**
> **Rests on a limb too slight.**
> **And feeling it gives way beneath him sings,**
> **Knowing he has wings.**
> (Streams in the Desert) L.B Cowman.

Chapter 11

❧ Giving ~ A Matter of ❧ the Heart

> **"I Give Myself Away"**
>
> *[Chorus:]*
> I give myself away
> I give myself away
> So You can use me
> I give myself away
> I give myself away
> So You can use me
>
> *[Verse 1:]*
> Here I am
> Here I stand
> Lord, my life is in your hands
> Lord, I'm longing to see
> Your desires revealed in me
> I give myself away
>
> *[Verse 2:]*
> Take my heart

> Take my life
> As a living sacrifice
> All my dreams all my plans
> Lord I place them in your hands
>
> *[Chorus:]*
> I give myself away
> I give myself away
> So You can use me
> I give myself away
> I give myself away
> So You can use me
>
> *[Bridge: x7]*
> My life is not my own
> To you I belong
> I give myself, I give myself to you
> By: William McDowell

HOW DO WE GIVE?

We are innately selfish beings. Early in a child's life, we see the tendency to be territorial; sets of behavior that we try earnestly to discourage. We teach our children to share, to give, to love, and to forgive, yet as they get older we discover that a prevailing characteristic tend to dominate their lifestyle; one of selfishness. How can we reconcile selfishness and giving?

To **give** is a simple concept and **giving** is a simple word. In the true heart of the word, when we **give** do we really achieve what it requires of us? Other words meaning **to give** include; to present, to hand, to help, to yield, to contribute, to distribute, to hand over or to part with. I particularly like this definition. Give means: *to bestow without receiving a return; to confer without compensation; to impart, as a possession; to grant as authority or permission; to yield up or allow ~ ARDictionary.*

If we really desire to reconcile our natural tendency of selfishness and what the true heart of giving is all about, we have to admit who we are and where our deficiencies are. Selfishness goes hand in hand with the opposite of giving.

Some antonyms to giving include; to hold, keep, take, withstand, challenge, deny, disallow, disapprove, oppose, refuse, withhold... How does our selfish nature accommodate the true heart of giving with our selfish tendencies? Both cannot coexist; we have to love one and hate the other.

IN THE CHURCH COMMUNITY

In the Church community, of course, we are taught to give of ourselves; to be benevolent. This is a traditional that has been embedded in our Church DNA that even when it is not officially taught, as in a class, we know it automatically. People in the Community will come to the Church in time of distress; in disasters people will find the Church for food and shelter; run-away-kids will try to find refuge in a Church, when they have exploited all other permissive options.

It is very good that there is this expectation. These occasions are opportunities to demonstrate the true heart of **Giving**; *to bestow without receiving in return and to confer without compensation.*

Lately, the lyrics of William McDowell's song *I give myself away* written above, has blessed me over and over and over again. I desire for God to use me and I long to see His desires revealed in me. I realize that to get to this place of utter abandonment before God, where I give myself away, requires self-sacrifice and selflessness. How many of us are really selfless? Not many; however we are called to selfless living; we are called to sacrifice ourselves ~ to give ourselves away, so God can use us.

"And so, dear brothers and sisters, I plead with you to give your bodies to God because of all he has done for you. Let them be a living and holy sacrifice—the kind he will find acceptable. This is truly the way to worship him. Don't copy the behavior and customs of this world, but let God transform you into a new person by changing the way you think. Then you will learn to know God's will for you, which is good and pleasing and perfect" (Romans 12:1-2) NLT.

God wants us to offer our lives as living sacrifices ~ daily laying aside our own desires to follow Him, putting all our energy and resources at His disposal and trusting Him to guide us. We do this out of gratitude that our Sins have been forgiven. God wants us to be transformed people with renewed minds, living to honor and obey Him. Because He wants only what is best for us, and because He gave His son to make our new life possible, we should joyfully give ourselves as living sacrifices for His service.

Paul warned the Romans *"don't copy the behavior and customs of this world"* that are usually selfish and corrupting. Our refusal to conform to this world's values, however, must go even deeper than just behaviors and customs; it must be firmly planted in the mind.

Let God transform you into a new person by changing the way you think. It is possible to avoid most worldly customs and still be proud, covetous, selfish, stubborn, and arrogant. Only when the Holy Spirit renews, reeducates, and redirects our minds are we truly transformed. <u>Life Application Study Bible</u> *Tyndale House Publishers, Inc.*

The Bible is replete with people who gave themselves totally to God. It was a struggle for all of them to come to a place of daily surrender to God. David went through his time of Sin and disobedience, even to the point of murder, before He cried out to God in absolute surrender (2 Samuel 11-12).

Paul persecuted the Church and scorned the very gospel that he eventually became zealous about. He was on his way to slaughter Christians as usual, but got turned around and became converted when he was confronted by God (Acts 9:1-3). Daniel had his own set of drama because of his commitment to God. He was thrown into a den of lions and survived to tell about it (Daniel 6).

Shadrach, Meshach, and Abednego had their concerns when facing the fiery consequences of their faith in God (Daniel 3). There and many others have great testimonies of a life given away to God who mightily used them. The same is required of you and me.

TITHING

Tithing has always been a sore point for both people in the Church Community as well as those in the World. Some reasons for this bone of contention include; lack of knowledge on the subject, selfishness and greed of parishioners, fleecing of members by crooked pastors, lack of trust of church leaders, to name a few. Dr Richard Fisher of Life Action Ministries and a professor of Moody Bible Institute wrote;

"The word tithe is one of the most powerful and controversial words in the church—its very mention can start a heated argument. Some believe it is part of the law of Christ (Galatians 6:2); the rest desperately hope that it was superseded by the New Covenant and has been abolished like the sacrificial system and the dietary laws!"

Regardless of your take on the concept of tithing, you will agree that it's worth the while to delve further and gain the truth of it. The first time the concept of tithing was mentioned in the Scriptures was in Genesis Chapter 14.

ABRAHAM AND MELCHIZEDEK

"Then Abram gave Melchizedek a tenth of all the goods he had recovered" (Genesis 14:20) NLT.

Abraham was on his way from rescuing his nephew Lot, when he ran into Melchizedeck king of Salem. Melchizedeck must have been a God-fearing man because his name means "king of righteousness" and king of Salem means "king of peace". The book of Hebrews chapter 7vs 1&2 refer to Melchizedeck as "priest of the most High God". So Melchizedeck blessed Abraham and in return Abraham gave him back one tenth or a tithe of all the good he recovered.

How did Abraham come up with this idea of giving back one tenth of what he got? Abraham was an idol worshipper before he committed himself to God. Even in some pagan religion, it was tradition to give one tenth of ones' earnings to the gods. Abraham followed accepted tradition. <u>Life Application Study Bible.</u>

Throughout the Old Testament we see where the people were required to bring a tithe of their earnings into the house of God. **"You must set aside a tithe of your crops—one-tenth of all the crops you harvest each year. Bring this tithe to the designated place of worship—the place the LORD your God chooses for his name to be honored—and eat it there in his presence. This applies to your tithes of grain, new wine, olive oil, and the firstborn males of your flocks and herds. Doing this will teach you always to fear the LORD your God"** (Deuteronomy 14: 22-23) NLT.

This practice was followed all the way up till Jesus introduced *grace,* unmerited favor that gives us a reprieve from the penalty of the law. Human beings could not live up to the total requirement of the law; in fact the Scriptures pointed out that if we were guilty of breaking one, we were then guilty of breaking all. **"For the person who keeps all of the laws except one is as guilty as a person who has broken all of God's laws"** (James 2:10) NLT.

But through grace, we have a favored position in Christ where God gives us the capacity to live above the law. Regarding Abraham, the father of faith this was said; **"God's promise to give the whole earth to Abraham and his descendants was based not on his obedience to God's law, but on a right relationship with God that comes by faith. If God's promise is only for those who obey the law, then faith is not necessary and the promise is pointless"** (Romans 4: 13-14) NLT.

So! We could not keep the law and grace came and grants us mercy, helping us to live a life of faith through which we receive the promise like Abraham did. Does it mean then that we quit trying to live in accordance to the law? Paul said *God forbid.*

"Well then, if we emphasize faith, does this mean that we can forget about the law? Of course not! In fact, only when we have faith do we truly fulfill the law" (Romans 3:31) NLT.

Let's go back to tithing. How does this apply? To the people who Dr Richard Fisher described regarding tithing as *"desperately hoping that it was superseded by the New Covenant and has been abolished like the sacrificial system and the dietary laws!"*

Here is further clarification. The books of 2 Corinthians 8-9 outline beautifully why we should give and how we aught to give.

- The people gave to help those who did not have
- They gave although they had needs themselves
- Their giving motivated other believers to give
- They gave willing beyond what was asked
- They gave cheerfully and generously
- Paul told them not to give out of pressure
- The amount given is not as important as why and how it is given
- Give out of love of God and dedication to the cause of Christ
- The Kingdom of God spread because of the believers concerns and eagerness to help others beyond their own circle of friends
- Linking up with other people of faith also increase Christian unity
- Giving is a natural response to love; Paul did not have to pump up the believers of Macedonia. He encouraged them to prove their love
- Giving is not limited to money and tangibles, but give of your time, talent and total self

- There is no evidence that Jesus was any poorer than any other Palestinian, rather Jesus became poor by giving up His right, so we may become rich in Him. He requires us to follow His example and give of ourselves
- Willingness to give enthusiastically is more importantly than the amount you give
- Give to fulfill your financial obligations
- Give to those in need, without expecting back in return; yet they might be the persons to help you in your time of need
- Give as a response to Christ, not for anything you can get out of it
- God give to us so we can give to others; give as the Lord prospers you
- Give of what you have, not what you do not have; your giving should not encroach on your family's basic needs

WHY WAS THE TITHE INSTITUTED?

The tithing system was a framework to facilitate a grateful and compassionate heart—a training program to help people love God and their neighbors. All the passages about tithing (even Malachi 3) focus on heart attitudes—on giving to facilitate community, equality, and support in times of need. God sees it as a discipline to encourage joy, thankfulness, and generosity, based on His own cheerful generosity and blessing. Dr Richard Fisher

The principle of tithing and emphasis on giving in the New Testament is obviously a matter of the heart. It seems then that we should endeavor to give far above the requirement of the law; not just in tangible things but in giving of ourselves. The rest of Dr. Foster article on Tithing was very helpful to me and I am sure it will help you too, so here I include it.

Is the tithe still part of God's program for giving?

If tithing is really the training instrument for a godly heart attitude, then setting it aside could be a serious mistake.

A recent survey conducted by the National Association of Evangelicals found that "42% of evangelical leaders believe the Bible requires tithing [for today], while 58% do not." Another study, by Empty Tomb, Inc. (a group that tracks church giving), found that "evangelicals on a whole give an average of 4% of their income [primarily] to their church."

However, Dan Olson, a Purdue University sociology professor who has studied tithing, suspects the average is much lower—around 1% or 2%. He explains why: "Most Christians would say the laws of the Old Testament are not what save you, you're supposed to be giving out of a spirit of freedom, not because you' rebound to laws."

But this raises some disconcerting questions: Why would a Spirit of Christian freedom lead the church, on average, to give less? Shouldn't New Covenant blessings and the "adult responsibility" of generous giving bring our average above that of Old Covenant believers? Wouldn't we expect obedient, cheerful givers to exceed the tithe?

Paul understood the heart of God underlying the tithing requirement. He took the tithing principles and applied them to the growing church in 2 Corinthians 8-9. One cannot read that passage without seeing the obvious references to Deuteronomy 12, 14-15, and 26.

However, Paul did not use the term *tithe*. He took the concept to the more responsible level, as addressing those who are no longer children but who now have the indwelling Spirit of God.

The concepts of generosity, of supporting God's work, of investing in people and the kingdom, and of doing God's will were used. Paul said that if we love God with all our hearts, we will give generously to the ministry; if we love our neighbors as ourselves, we will give generously to assist them as we are able.

Paul also raised the bar when he said that the ***Corinthians* "gave themselves first to the Lord and then to us in keeping with God's will" (2 Cor. 8:5).**

> We no longer need to concentrate on some minimum requirement to satisfy God, like a child would; rather, we should be giving 100% of ourselves to Him.

We who love Christ are not satisfied, now that we have experienced the full love of God, to give just a tithe; we want to give it all.

Tithing can be used to train children to have a generous heart and to invest in God's work. This is what God did with Israel. But that's only a temporary measure; as part of the Mosaic Law, it was only a shadow of better things to come in the New Covenant (Galatians 3:19-25).

Giving 10% is a starting place, a discipline for beginners. As we mature in faith, we grow beyond the rule and learn to cheerfully say, "Everything I have is Yours. I want to be a channel through which Your blessings flow. I will use Your money where it is most needed. Guide me with Your wisdom." Dr. Richard Fisher has served as a professor and regional director with Moody Bible Institute.

THE TITHE IN THE BIBLE

1. *Genesis 14:18-20*
2. *Leviticus 27:30-33*
3. *Numbers 18:8-21*
4. *Deuteronomy12:6-7;14:22-28;26:1- 15*
5. *2 Chronicles 31:5-12*
6. *Nehemiah 10:35-39; 12:44; 13:4-13*
7. *Malachi 3:8-12*
8. *Matthew 23:23-24*
9. *Luke 11:42*
10. *Hebrews 7:1-10*

It is good to discover that there is a higher purpose for living beyond the mundane activities of working to buy things, spending and never seeming to be satisfied, and consuming all that's acquired in life. The book of Proverbs admonishes us:

"Do not withhold good from those who deserve it when it's in your power to help them. If you can help your neighbor now, don't say, "Come back tomorrow, and then I'll help you" (Proverbs 3: 27-28) NLT.

"If you help the poor, you are lending to the LORD— and he will repay you!" (Proverbs 19:17) NLT.

"If your enemies are hungry, give them food to eat. If they are thirsty, give them water to drink" (Proverbs 25:21) NLT.

These are only a few of the many Scriptures that encourage us to give of ourselves. It is a learning process for me and I am being challenged every day to share my life with others. I aim to inspire and encourage others to do the same.

BIOGRAPHY

Venoris Patten is a unique person who embraces the circumstances of her life, endeavoring to see the true purpose of each occurrence. She has come into this awareness over a period of time as she reflected on the journey of her entire life and started questioning the purpose of certain events.

She is the fourth of ten siblings and grew up in a traditional home with mom, dad and siblings. She is the proud mother of two sons and five grandchildren.

Venoris earned her nursing diploma at the University of the West Indies Jamaica, West Indies and later achieved her Bachelors and Masters degrees in Health Services Administration at Florida International University, Miami Florida.

Venoris is passionate about encouraging others and works diligently within the Church and lately the neighboring community to give support to others. She believes strongly in one encouraging the other. She volunteers with America Cancer Society, Esther's Outreach Ministry, and is a mentor at "New Beginnings" bringing spiritual, emotional and physical support to the local community.

Her autobiography, "Nuggets...along the Way" and now her 2nd book "Putting away Childish Things" are recent literary accomplishments. Not only are they legacies for her family and especially her children and grandchildren, but serve as means of sharing her life with a wider audience. She hopes to encourage all to seek purpose because she believes that living a purpose filled life is the key to real freedom and fulfillment.

Proceeds from her autobiography are invested into LifeShare Ministries, Inc., her recently established non-profit, community – based organization that exists simply to affirm and empower young women. The aim is to identify, secure, affirm, and educate "at risk" and abused girls and abused women bringing them to a place of wellness, wholeness and purpose.

www.ingramcontent.com/pod-product-compliance
Lightning Source LLC
Chambersburg PA
CBHW032115090426
42743CB00007B/361